W9-ACL-666

ECONOMIC POLICIES FOR THE NEW HUNGARY: PROPOSALS FOR A COHERENT APPROACH

by

Otto Hieronymi

with the participation of an
International Group of Experts

Copy Donated By

Battelle
. . . Putting Technology To Work

BATTELLE PRESS
Columbus • Richland

Library of Congress Cataloging-in-Publication Data

Hieronymi, Otto.
    Economic policies for the new Hungary: proposals for
a coherent approach/by Otto Hieronymi; with participation
of an international group of experts.

        p.   cm.
    ISBN 0-935470-60-3 : $18.95
    1. Hungary—Economic policy—1989–   2. Hungary—Economic
conditions—1989–   3. Hungary—Foreign economic relations.
I. Title.
HC300.282.H54   1990   90-36278
338.9439—dc20   CIP

Printed in the United States of America.

Copyright©1990, Battelle Memorial Institute

All rights reserved. No part of this book may be reproduced or transmitted in any form or
by any means, electronic or mechanical, including photocopying, recording or by any information storage and retrieval system, without permission from the publisher.

Battelle Press
505 King Avenue
Columbus, Ohio 43201-2693
614-424-6393
1-800-451-3543
Fax: 614-424-5263

PREFACE

The present study was undertaken on the initiative of Battelle Europe, with the financial support of the Swiss government. The study was prepared by Battelle Europe, with the active participation of a Western group of experts. The members of this group who participated in a personal capacity and not as representatives of their respective organizations, represent a broad spectrum of national backgrounds and professional experience. The publication of this study in English and Hungarian was made possible by a grant from the Jacobs Suchard Foundation.

The principal objectives of this study are listed below:

1. Present a brief, independent analysis of the economic, financial, monetary, and social prospects of Hungary.

2. Review the policies being followed and proposed in Hungary.

3. Consider the precedents and policy models that could be followed in the transformation of the Hungarian economy.

4. Identify the short- and long-term domestic and external risks and opportunities.

5. Formulate recommendations for policies that Hungary and its foreign partners ought to follow for the successful transformation and modernization of the Hungarian economy, to achieve sustained growth and higher living standards, and to allow Hungary to meet its external obligations.

This study does not aim to be an academic analysis or a consensus report. Although the members of the group generally agree on the principal issues and recommendations, the author alone is responsible for the final wording of the report. The Swiss government is not responsible for the form, the contents, or the recommendations of the present report.

The original idea for a brief independent analysis dealing with the Hungarian economy and with the need for a coherent policy approach was formulated following a roundtable discussion hosted by the Hungarian government in Budapest in late September 1989. This meeting on the current economic situation and policies of Hungary also included about a dozen Western experts who participated in the discussion in a private capacity.

The 1989 roundtable discussion followed two earlier seminars, hosted by the Hungarian National Bank and the Hungarian Academy of Sciences in 1986 and 1988 at Szirak Castle, that dealt with the evolution of the international monetary system. Several of the Western participants at the Budapest Round Table had also attended the Szirak meetings.

The discussions in Budapest showed that it would be useful for present and future Hungarian decision makers to have an independent outside assessment of the prospects for the Hungarian economy and of recommendations concerning the short- and long-term priorities for economic, financial, and monetary policies in the domestic and international areas. Furthermore, there is also considerable need for information and systematic analyses of the Hungarian economy in the OECD countries and for independent recommendations for policies to be followed toward Hungary.

In addition to the discussions and to the information obtained at the Budapest Round Table, this report draws on a series of in-depth discussions with Hungarian experts, and opposition leaders and economists in late November and early December 1989, on conversations with experts and officials in a number of OECD countries and international organizations, as well as on extensive documentation on the Hungarian reform debate and the Hungarian economy.

Following are the members of the group who provided input for the present report:

Peter J. Bull
  Société Générale Strauss Turnbull Securities, London
Emilio Fontela,
  Professor, University of Geneva and University of Madrid
Otto Hieronymi,
  Battelle Geneva Research Centers, Geneva
Alfonso Jozzo,
  Banco San Paolo di Torino, Turin
Nicolas Krul,
  Geneva and Ménerbes, France

Laszlo Nagy,
   President, Jacobs Suchard Foundation, Geneva
Wilhelm Nölling,
   President, Landeszentralbank Hamburg
Jean-Pierre Roth,
   Director, Swiss National Bank, Zurich
Tsuneaki Sato,
   Professor, Nihon University, Tokyo
Robert Solomon,
   Brookings Institution, Washington, D.C.
Miklos Szabo-Pelsöczi,
   President, GlobalConsult, Bedford, New York, and Budapest
Paul Tar,
   Banque Nationale de Paris, Paris
Franz-Josef Trouvain,
   Chief Economist and Executive Vice President, Deutsche Bank, Frankfurt.

This report was completed at the end of January 1990. Only minor modifications were made in the original text. The report was distributed to the OECD governments, to the major international economic organizations, and to past and future officials in Hungary. In a series of discussions held in Hungary and in the OECD countries, including Japan, the report and its recommendations were received with considerable interest. The developments since last January, and especially the speed and direction of developments in favor of East Germany, confirm the validity of the analysis and of the relevance of the recommendations presented in this report. They also underscore the urgency to act upon them.

SUMMARY OF PRINCIPAL CONCLUSIONS AND RECOMMENDATIONS

The present study was prepared by Battelle Europe with the participation of an international group of experts. Its main objective is to present a series of policy recommendations in view of creating the basis for sustained growth and the integration of Hungary into the European and world economies in the 1990s.

Hungary is in the process of breaking with the rules and structures of the Socialist economy and of creating the conditions for the development of a dynamic market economy. The aim is to release the productive forces of the Hungarian population, to stimulate private initiative, and to increase the weight of the existing small private sector. There is a need for competition, liberalization, the diffusion of new technologies, and extensive structural change throughout the economy. There is a broad scope for foreign direct investments in Hungary and for joint ventures and cooperation between large and small Hungarian and foreign companies.

Today Hungary suffers from the consequences of the virtual economic stagnation of the 1980s, from double-digit inflation, and from a heavy external debt burden. There is a need for fiscal and monetary discipline and for a more realistic price structure. Austerity policies, however, are not enough, especially not if they provide a powerful boost to inflation, as was the case with the government's latest program adopted at the end of 1989. There is a need for balanced growth to raise living standards and to renew and to upgrade productive and infrastructure capital. It is of the utmost importance to assure the careful and economic use of the private and official resource transfer.

Agenda for Action

It is only by adopting a well-defined and integrated set of goals and policies, to be carried out with determination, that the economic transformation can succeed and the vicious circle of stagnation and rising external debt burden

be broken. To design and to implement such a program, a coherent approach
and the close cooperation of the Hungarian authorities and of the Organization for Economic Cooperation and Development (OECD) countries are
indispensable. The five sets of principal recommendations proposed in this
report constitute such an integrated concept. They are presented with a sense
of urgency to Hungarians and to decision makers in the OECD countries.

1   **A "grand design" for balanced growth, international economic in-
    tegration and the development of a modern market economy in
    Hungary**
    The first task is to adopt a realistic "grand design" for the Hun-
garian economy. This should command the broad support of the
people and provide a basic, stable framework for both private initiative
and for policy makers. It should put an end to the practice of constant
tinkering with economic policies and structures and should help dispel
the current uncertainty and confusion about long-term economic
objectives, risks and priorities. This grand design should contain the
basic goals for growth and increased prosperity, and for the transformation of the Hungarian economy into a modern, liberal market
economy. It should define the role of the State, the protection of
economic freedom and of private property, the need for domestic and
external stability, for effective social policies and for increased international economic integration. It should identify the necessary policy
tools and contain a realistic timetable. This "grand design" could find
inspiration in the successful economic policies of the Western European countries and in the European tradition of the "social market
economy" (not to be confused with "market socialism" or with the
"welfare state").

2   **A joint task force of officials from Hungary and the OECD countries
    to promote Hungary's integration into the world economy**
    Increased economic integration and cooperation with the OECD
countries is a major challenge for Hungary. It is essential to organize
the common effort and to avoid waste of scarce human and material
resources. To identify needs and resources, to increase the effectiveness
of technical and material assistance, to help channel advice and technology transfer, a temporary "Task Force Hungary" should be created
at the earliest possible date. Its mandate should not exceed three years.
It should be headquartered in Budapest. Its small, full-time staff should
include Hungarians and officials from other national administrations
and from international organizations.

3   **A Hungarian-International long-term credit and development bank for an optimum utilization of the resource transfer**

The creation of a Hungarian-International Bank, which would co-operate closely with the planned Bank for European Reconstruction and Development (BERD) and existing institutions, but which would concentrate on Hungarian problems and also act as a "counterpart fund," is essential for the success of the reform of the Hungarian monetary, banking, and financial system, and to avoid a wasteful use of the public and private resource transfer. The goal is not to increase the flow of funds into Hungary beyond the level possible under current arrangements, but to increase its effectiveness. The Bank should aim at promoting private enterprise (in particular small and medium-sized companies), productive infrastructure investments, and the protection of the environment. It should also play an active role in the consolidation of the banking and financial system, and in the management of Hungary's external debt. The creation of this Bank, which would have an initial Western majority control, should coincide with the consolidation and reform of the central bank and of the Hungarian banking system and with the conclusion of a long-term debt-adjustment program.

4   **Negotiating a long-term debt-adjustment program**

The conclusion of a negotiated debt-adjustment program is a vital necessity for the success the Hungarian economy. Thus, it is also in the interest of its creditors and, in general, of the OECD countries. It is essential to reduce, for at least the next three years, the volume of interest payments by Hungary. Without debt adjustment it would be illusory to expect an effective implementation of the other measures. Austerity policies would be an exercise in political futility. They would not guarantee a return to growth, and thus the country's capacity to honor its external financial obligations. Debt adjustment, however, must not be wasted. That is why it has to be closely linked with the proposed Hungarian-International Bank and with the consolidation of the National Bank and the financial system.

5   **Controlling inflation, promoting private property and competition, and completing the reform of the National Bank**

The problem of inflation must not be taken lightly, as has been the case in the recent past. Without checking inflation there will be no room for broadening convertibility. An effective antiinflationary policy requires the creation of a strong central bank, which would

be charged with maintaining monetary stability and would be autonomous from Parliament and the government. It is also necessary to
have a flexible, but effective, wage and price policy. Promoting savings
and private capital formation, and creating respect for private property,
are essential for the success of the market economy. These principles
should be applied consistently in the privatization program, which
has to be a long-term process in order to avoid waste and corruption.
Competition and responsible management are the bases of a market
economy. In State-owned companies market pressure should be
allowed to work as much as possible. Until a gradual privatization
program is designed and implemented, the State must not abdicate
the owner's ultimate responsibility for controlling the efficient and
careful management of its property.

TABLE OF CONTENTS

ECONOMIC POLICIES FOR THE NEW HUNGARY: PROPOSALS FOR A COHERENT APPROACH

CHALLENGES, RISKS, AND OPPORTUNITIES

An Historic Opportunity

In the 1990s, domestic and external circumstances could favor the development of a free social, political, and economic order in Hungary, which could provide the basis for the sustained growth of the Hungarian economy. Such an opportunity has been the central aspiration of Hungarians since at least the 1940s. Along with wide-ranging liberalization in the domestic sphere, political independence and closer international cooperation begin to seem possible.

At the same time, the situation in the countries of the Organization for Economic Cooperation and Development (OECD) is exceptionally favorable for Hungary. The political and ethical interests and the economic and financial interests of the industrialized countries are converging in Hungary's favor. European integration will help Hungary overcome a number of external problems and traditional friction points.

Success will not come automatically. There are only a few ways of doing things right and many possibilities for error. Hungary will need to steer a tight course between continuity and flexibility. This study concludes that the chances of success are real. If the right policies are pursued in Hungary and abroad, the Hungarian case may bring major economic, political, and social rewards beyond the country's borders.

The historic and promising character of recent political changes must not be underestimated. For decades Westerners and most Hungarians have considered these changes to be the preconditions of successful economic reform.

Two areas of political uncertainty remain:

- Political destabilization in the Soviet Union and in Eastern Europe

- Difficulties with the political transformation in Hungary, parliamentary instability, and the lack of consensus about the future of the country.

However, the abandonment of the Communist economic system, which had never enjoyed real popular support, has fostered broad agreement in Hungary about the need for fundamental changes and about the general direction and nature of these changes.

■ Challenges and Opportunities

Economic reform in Hungary has great potential but faces some formidable challenges. It can raise living standards closer to those which a highly capable and industrious people can expect, but some of the necessary changes run counter to strongly entrenched and powerful interests. For more than 40 years, Hungarians have been subjected to extensive state control and have only limited experience of a market economy. The dangers arise because unsuccessful or unacceptable reforms not only can result in economic hardship, but also can invite social and political backlash. Substantial economic reform will be a much more complex and long-term process than political reform.

Nevertheless, the 1990s promise sustained growth, improved living standards, an accumulation of savings and private property, as well as an improved quality of life.

Since many of the crucial economic indicators are either very low, or distorted, a change in the economic climate and in the basic objectives and policy framework, and the introduction of appropriate incentives throughout the economy can bring about relatively important and visible productivity improvements. Quantitative improvement ought to be obtained from a more efficient use of resources. This could be boosted by qualitative changes resulting from a stable and predictable political, economic, and social framework and from a more market-oriented supply of goods and services.

Cutting back on waste will reduce shortages in the economy. Since the demand for most products and services is not saturated, there should be considerable opportunities for creating new markets provided there is a will to seek out customers and to satisfy them.

Trial and error—and failure—are part of the economic process. Among the most serious defects of the Socialist economy are its subordination of efficiency and welfare to ideology and its tendency not to recognize or admit errors or failures. The larger the project, the greater this reluctance and the greater its cost. A market-driven economy offers an efficient early warning system, allowing unsuccessful endeavors to be intercepted early. One of the most encouraging and most positive features of the market economy is the possibility to start again.

This feature, however, does not offer unlimited room for social and economic experimentation. Long-term goals and a basic framework have to be clearly defined. Economic reform and economic policies take time to achieve their full impact. The temptation to tinker with the system, which has characterized Socialist economic reform and management, has to be avoided both by Hungarian leaders and decision makers and by their Western counterparts and advisers.

The Starting Point: The Need to Overcome Pessimism Itself

Although the current international situation is characterized by rapid change and considerable volatility, the favorable domestic and external constellation facing Hungary today could hardly have been imagined as recently as eight or twelve months ago.

Nevertheless, many opinions and analyses from within Hungary on its economic prospects are marked by profound pessimism. Numerous publications, articles, interviews, speeches, and radio and television programs reflect a widespread preoccupation with the country's immediate and long-term economic outlook. Pessimism seemed to have increased considerably, even when compared with a period as recent as the autumn of 1989.

A number of developments here contributed to this underlying pessimism:

- General political uncertainties

- The decline or stagnation of the real income of much of the population

- The announcement of a severe austerity program

- Widespread realization of the debt problem and the fear of its impact on Hungary's modernization and growth

- Fear of the failure of Soviet reform and of a subsequent backlash that could affect Hungary

- Relatively slow change in the real economy, compared with the substantial changes "on paper"

- Substantial price increases for basic goods (meat, rent, transportation) and growing fear of inflation

- Fear of unemployment

- A feeling of inadequacy resulting from the general technology gap between today's Hungary and the OECD countries

- Apprehension that the entrenched rulers were trying to save their privileges and are maneuvering to retain power

- The proliferation of opposition parties and the vocal dissension among their leaders

- Unfamiliarity with a market economy and apprehension about adjusting to it

- Confusion about the privatization program and fears of speculative capital imports (*Ausverkauf der Heimat**)

- The rescinding of foreign exchange travel allowances

- Constant warnings of economic difficulties and pessimistic comments by the former government about the general economic and political situation.

One of the main sources of pessimism has been the lack of a coherent vision about the future economic order in Hungary. Despite wide-ranging debate, people are confused about the challenges, the external and domestic opportunities facing Hungary, and about the policies required to take advantage of these opportunities. The speed with which the ruling party appears to have moved from "reform Socialism" toward an apparently "orthodox monetarist" economic philosophy, and the haste with which it has been pushing fundamental legislation through Parliament, have added considerably to the confusion about the possibilities and advantages of economic reform.

Although outside observers share this sense of confusion, their general perception is that Hungary stands a better chance of succeeding in its attempt at gradually becoming a dynamic market economy than several of the other Eastern European countries, especially the Soviet Union. This is partly because of Hungary's courageous and pragmatic attempts at economic reform since 1968 and more recently at political reform. Despite the piecemeal nature of many economic measures and the numerous errors committed, throughout the 1970s and 1980s Hungary compared very favorably with the quality of economic thinking and management in the other Socialist countries. Hungary is distinguished by the presence of a well-educated middle class, with an existing commercial culture, and of a fairly skilled working class. The fact that momentous political and societal changes have taken place without a domestic and external economic and financial breakdown (and without the related extreme social hardships and waste that accompany them), also speaks in favor of the future success of the Hungarian economy.

Despite the obvious shortcomings of the various reform programs and the numerous errors of economic management, the Hungarian example has catalyzed the deep political, economic, and societal changes taking place in the Communist world. The example of a certain limited economic freedom and of a certain economic rationality (and ultimately the limited results of partial reform, mostly in agriculture, cooperative, and private industrial and

---

*"Selling out the fatherland" to foreign interests.

service ventures) have influenced current thinking in the Soviet Union and in the other Eastern European countries.

Although Hungary's Parliamentary majority and government did not change until the Spring of 1990, it was the only Eastern European country where the first free elections in well over 40 years were being planned in an orderly manner and where no mass demonstrations and disruptive strikes had been necessary to force the ruling party to abandon its political monopoly and share power.

Moreover, notwithstanding the obvious domestic and external economic difficulties, Hungary stands out as the Eastern European country most able to avoid economic, financial, and social breakdown. Despite the evident signs of increased inflationary pressure, there has been no inflationary explosion and subsequent flight into goods and Western currencies. Hungarian authorities rightly recognized that a dollarization of the Hungarian economy would not be an auspicious beginning either for the domestic market economy or for the independence and external creditworthiness of the country. They have been anxious to maintain the country's international credit standing. Maintaining the integrity and continuity of domestic policy-making and some level of confidence in the national currency will serve Hungary well through the changes ahead. The *tabula rasa* or "scorched earth" approach to economic reform is bad economics; its advocacy is based largely on a misreading of history and especially of the evidence of postwar reconstruction in Western Europe.

However serious the challenges of transforming and modernizing the Hungarian economy, it is not broken down: production, inflation, the supply and availability of goods, and foreign trade, and the balance of payments remain reasonably healthy, and at least for the time being the tolerance and anticipated consensus of the Hungarian people can be expected. The government will have to work hard to maintain foreign and domestic confidence. Conversely, Western countries will find it in their economic and political interest to help Hungary overcome short-term difficulties and to cooperate with the country in its long-term development.

The magnitude of the task must not be underestimated. The economic structure remains inefficient and in many ways obsolete, and there is considerable resistance to change (or apprehension of the risks inherent in change) in all sectors of the economy—in industry, agriculture, services, and especially in the bureaucracy. People resist giving up the traditional privileges of office, and many of them find it difficult to change ingrained ways of doing things. The habit of expecting changes to come "from above" and then cleverly circumventing them is an inheritance from the old system.

Qualitative changes should be swift and evident. The design and implementation of reforms should follow a gradual but consistent path. The haste with which the government has been trying to push through reforms in the economic structure appears to have led, in many instances, to a new appearance, but little substantive change.

In the current economic climate and the coming period of transition, the fight against inflation—and the monopolies that amplify it—must be taken seriously. The economic and social hardships that would result from continued high inflation, and especially the possible threat of a runaway inflation, can hardly be overstated; neither should the memory of postwar Hungarian inflation (which statistically exceeded even the great German inflation of the 1920s) be taken lightly or forgotten. This inflation wiped out the personal savings of the entire Hungarian population, preparing the ground for the Communist economic takeover. Any political backlash to current economic reform would likely result from the hardships created by inflation.

Despite the lively debate about privatization, evidence suggests that relatively little has been done to expand the already existing private economy—the so-called gray or shadow economy—in Hungary. Reducing the mostly bureaucratic obstacles to the growth of this genuine and spontaneous entrepreneurship (including the lack of bank credit from which it has been suffering from the start) is as important a task as the planned privatization of State-owned companies (which often involves the sale of other state-owned firms or banks).

This report reflects the general debate on the reform prospects of Hungary and other Eastern European countries on monetary and financial issues. Yet, the most fundamental changes have to take place on the "real" side of the economy: who commands in the economy? Bureaucrats and party officials, or the markets, consumers, and entrepreneurs? An effective market economy will have to bring about changes in production structures and incentives; increase mobility, motivation, and productivity of labor; reduce red tape; and facilitate the redistribution of resources, the diffusion of modern technologies, competition, and broadly based private initiatives.

The experience of numerous countries in the 1970s and the 1980s has shown once more that inflation and monetary disorders have a negative impact, and domestic and external stability a positive one, on economic performance. But recent economic history has also demonstrated that, without important changes on the real side of the economy, without new incentives and motivations, fiscal and monetary discipline become sterile austerity, which by itself cannot create the basis for sustained and balanced growth.

It is important to emphasize the character of this historic opportunity both for Hungary and for the Western world. The convergence is unique of domestic and international interests in the success of the transformation of the Hungarian economy and the creation of the basis for sustained and balanced economic growth in the 1990s. Sustained and balanced economic growth ought to be the underlying theme of the new government's economic program and of international economic cooperation.

AN AGENDA FOR ACTION

For two decades Hungary has undertaken the most systematic attempts to reform the Socialist economic system. Hungary was the first among the Eastern European countries to recognize the futility of partial reforms, and the first to embark on a course consisting of a peaceful but radical break with an economic order imposed from the outside 40 years earlier. This report concludes that, on the whole, the on-going evolution in Hungary and the policies of the OECD countries toward Hungary are on the right track. Some corrections are required, and the need is urgent to focus more sharply on the key issues and reinforce the main lines of change.

Economic and social policies have to be closely tailored to the situation and structure of each country. Their current situations and the structural problems differ in important ways. Thus, in formulating the economic policies of Hungary and of the OECD countries, it is important to keep in mind the specific conditions in each country with respect to internal structures, policies, and macroeconomic equilibrium. Applying identical policies in Poland, Hungary, or East Germany (DDR) would be economically erroneous and socially and politically counterproductive. The successful transformation and integration of Hungary and other Eastern European countries cannot be carried out in isolation, on a bilateral basis, without an efficient multilateral approach. The example of the major contributions in the 1950s of the Organization for European Economic Cooperation (OEEC) and of the European Payments Union ought to be remembered in this context. These two organizations, in the framework of the Marshall Plan, played an essential role in the reconstruction of the European economies and in making possible their international integration. Without them there would have been no European economic integration.

Defining and adopting a coherent program in the coming months is essential to the successful transformation of the Hungarian economy into a dynamic market economy in the 1990s. Such a program will have to consider the progress achieved so far, and set clear goals and priorities for action in Hungary and for its relations with the OECD countries. It must be based on a realistic and pragmatic approach, incorporating a careful evaluation of the risks involved and a commonly agreed timetable. Caution is as critical as bold decisions.

The conclusions of this report are formulated in five sets of interdependent recommendations. They are urgently addressed to Hungarians and to decision makers in the OECD countries. Planning should start on all five simultaneously at the earliest possible date.

1   **A "grand design" for balanced growth, international economic integration, and the development of a modern market economy in Hungary**

This "grand design" has to define clearly the long-term objectives for the Hungarian economy and the major steps necessary to attain them. It should distinguish between the basic characteristics of the system, the institutional changes and policy instruments required, and the initial policy measures that have to be adopted. It should conform to Hungarian aspirations and take into account the lessons from the economic and social success of the OECD countries since the World War II. Thus, Hungarian leaders could find inspiration in the Western European tradition of the "social market economy" (not to be confused with the "welfare state" or with "democratic socialism") and in the policies that have been responsible for the new growth and new confidence in Europe in the 1980s, following an extended period of slow growth and widespread "Europessimism."

2   **A joint task force of officials from Hungary and the OECD countries to promote Hungary's integration into the world economy**

This temporary task force will help organize cooperation between the OECD countries and Hungary and assist in the transformation of Hungary's economy and its integration into the European and international economy. Its mandate and mode of operation ought to be patterned after the postwar OEEC. Although its tasks would be focused on Hungarian problems, it would be closely integrated with the ongoing and increased cooperation between the Eastern European countries and the rest of the world.

3   **A Hungarian-International Long-Term Credit and Development Bank for the optimum utilization of resource transfer**

This new bank should be jointly set up by OECD governments, creditor banks, the Hungarian government, and the Hungarian

National Bank. The first two groups should have temporary majority control. Its principal task would be to promote efficient macroeconomic and microeconomic use of the resource transfer to Hungary through both private and official channels. The bank should also play the role of a counterpart fund. It would closely cooperate with the new Bank for European Reconstruction and Development (BERD) and with other international organizations*, foreign governments, and banks. The creation of this bank, to be carried out simultaneously with the reform of the central bank, is a key element in the overhaul of the Hungarian financial system.

4 **A negotiated, long-term debt-adjustment program**

The central objective of the debt-adjustment program, as of the other recommendations, is to contribute to the successful transformation of the Hungarian economy and to the creation of the conditions for stable and sustained growth. Such a program, to be negotiated with Hungary's new leaders, will benefit both Hungary and its foreign private and official creditors.

5 **Controlling inflation, promoting private property and competition, and completing the reform of the National Bank**

The austerity program adopted at the end of 1989 has added dangerously to inflationary pressures through sharp price rises in basic commodities and services. A long-term anti-inflationary program is needed that is not limited to macroeconomic (monetary and fiscal) policies. In an economy where markets are far from functioning efficiently, an anti-inflationary policy has to incorporate effective price and wage surveillance. A central element of this program should be the transformation of the Hungarian National Bank into a modern central bank, which would be responsible for domestic and external monetary stability and would be autonomous with respect to both the government and the Parliament. Private initiative, competition, and genuine private capital formation are critical to Hungary's success, as is the efficient management of the numerous State-owned companies. Privatization has to be recognized as a complex process, to be carefully managed over a number of years.

The aim of the five principal recommendations, as the rest of the report, is not originality, as such. They reflect the thinking in Hungary and in the OECD countries with respect to Hungary. However, the urgency of implementing them cannot be overstated.

---

*Including the International Monetary Fund (IMF), the International Bank for Reconstruction and Development (IBRD, also called the World Bank), and the International Finance Corporation (IFC).

1 A "Grand Design" for Balanced Growth, International Economic Integration, and the Development of a Modern Market Economy in Hungary

LONG-TERM GOALS AND THE SEARCH FOR ECONOMIC MODELS

The first task for Hungary's leaders is to define a set of consistent long-term objectives to explain, justify, and sustain the structural changes being proposed and the policies to be carried out. Such a "grand design" should define the main issues and priorities within a realistic time-frame. It is needed both to generate broad consensus and sustained political support around a predictable line of development, and to serve as a basis in the formulation of economic policies.

A clear view of the direction in which Hungary is heading is also necessary to build confidence among Hungary's foreign partners, among others, to promote long-term investment.

It is evident that no foreign economic model could or should be directly imported into Hungary, for both practical and political reasons. Neither would it be reasonable to impose a rigid prescription for economic recovery and for the creation of a competitive market economy. Hungary is neither a developing country nor a modern industrialized economy. No precedents now exist yet of the successful transformation of a Socialist economy into a dynamic market economy.

Two broad perspectives will help to answer the questions that all Hungarians are asking today: Why has Hungary fared less well since the war than the Western European countries? What lessons from our history can be applied to future Hungarian economic policies? These two perspectives speak to the general factors responsible for the exceptional growth and integration of the world economy since the 1940s, and the identification of specific models of successful countries or groups of countries in economic reform and in the development of economic and social policies.

THE MAINSPRINGS OF ECONOMIC PROSPERITY SINCE THE 1940s

The last 40 years have seen unequalled growth and prosperity throughout much of the world economy. Among the principal factors responsible for this exceptional performance, the following deserve particular emphasis:

- *The gradual freeing of the movement of goods, labor, capital, and services among the principal trading nations* and increasingly among the so-called developing countries, which has led to an unprecedented degree of international economic, financial, and technological integration and to great improvements in resource allocation

- *The benefits and effective workings of competition markets and the fairly full utilization of productive resources,* which were bolstered by market opportunities and specialization, and by the joint financing facilitated by international economic integration

- *The rapid and largely unhampered diffusion of new and modern technologies* at the level of product design and production techniques, as well as efficient methods of organization and management (including the adoption of advanced sectorial models in manufacturing, agriculture, and services)

- *The development of a close network of regional and worldwide international economic cooperation* and joint management on both official and private levels, along with improved policy insight and management practices.

These four factors are expected to continue to stimulate economic growth during the 1990s and beyond, not only in Western Europe, but throughout the world. One of the principal deterrants to economic development in Eastern Europe during the last 40 years has been the inability to participate fully in the above developments.

The partial attempts by Hungary during the 1970s and 1980s to correct this situation have been largely responsible for its relative prosperity compared with the other Communist countries. It can also be argued that current technological developments, as well as the general globalization of factor, product, and service markets, will increase the benefits of participating in these trends, and conversely, they will increase the difficulties and the economic penalties of attempts at autarchy and economic nationalism.

Today, there is broad agreement in Hungary and abroad that the chances of the country's future economic success are closely linked to its ability to catch up with the rest of the world with respect to the above four factors of economic growth. Thus, the long-term objective should be an open economy that participates fully in regional and worldwide markets. This objective will require patience and highly consistent domestic policies. Economic integration helps re-enforce domestic economic discipline and economic rationality, but without a domestic effort its advantages cannot be realized.

Economic isolation and economic nationalism carry a very heavy price even for the largest countries. However, international economic integration does not imply that countries, whether large or small, should surrender their national identity or control over their resources and prosperity. It does require, at the policy level and at the level of households and companies, an attitude that balances competition with cooperation and solidarity.

HUNGARY AND THE WESTERN EUROPEAN EXPERIENCE WITH THE "SOCIAL MARKET ECONOMY"

Successful international economic integration requires appropriate domestic policies. This study concludes that the experiences most directly relevant to Hungary are those of the Western European countries, both in the postwar reconstruction period and during more recent decades:

- The reforms and policies enacted in Western Europe were and continue to be successful. They have resulted in the spectacular economic achievements of the last 40 years, as well as the equally remarkable individual freedom, social progress and stability achieved during this period in most of these countries.

- The European countries are the most open economies in the world. This has been achieved periodically within the European Community and the European Free Trade Association (EFTA), which have reduced economic barriers to trade and investment and have promoted and facilitated greater competition and economic dynamism. In this process, they have also faced complex foreign and domestic compromises. On the whole, they have succeeded in maintaining their national identities and internal structures, while developing an unprecedented degree of cooperation and integration of their economies and in many areas of decision making.

- Both smaller and larger European economies have been, for the most part, open to external experience or external models. During the last 40 years, European economies and European companies have learned from overseas experiences in the United States and Canada and in Japan and Korea, and they continue to do so.

- The general aspirations of most Hungarians align with the Western European model. However great the differences may be between Hungary and the various Western European countries, the European experience is likely to be the most easily accessible in terms of political, cultural, and social affinity.

The most successful model of economic reform and policies common to the Western European countries can be best described under the term, "social market economy." Because of the sometimes inaccurate use of this term in the current Hungarian election campaign; clarification is in order. The social market economy is fundamentally different in its objectives and instruments than any of the various forms of Socialism, including the concept of the "socialist market economy" (an idea that had been used until recently in the Eastern European countries, particularly in Hungary, to describe partial reforms of the Socialist economic system). Nor is the social market economy identical with the "welfare state," a concept that tends to emphasize redistribution or distribution of wealth and income, often at the expense of the level, efficiency, and composition of output. There is, however, a broad consensus about the main aspects of the social market economy among most Socialist and Conservative parties in Western Europe today. The social market economy is an open and liberal market economy based on the principles of economic freedom, individual effort, and private property. It differs, however, from the pure 19th century concept of the market economy in its recognition that all economic and social functions cannot be fulfilled properly by the market, and that some markets do not work efficiently.

Thus, there is an important division of labor between the market and the state. The state (whether at the national, regional, or local level) has to assume some important functions, not only to assure genuine, fair, and effective competition and, thereby, the proper working of markets, but also to assure social justice (which is not an attempt to create equality or an egalitarian society) and to help correct distortions that may result from competition and from market functioning.

This division of labor between the state and the markets has to be organized in a pragmatic manner according to the specific conditions and preferences of each country. It is subject to change under the influence of changing economic conditions and political preferences. Although this division of labor still operates at the national level in European countries, it has also taken on an increasingly Europe-wide dimension. An example of the flexibility and adaptability of the concept is the current trend toward deregulation and privatization in Western Europe.

A successful market economy must balance two forces:

- *Stability*—Political freedom, the rule of law and a stable legal framework, monetary stability, the protection of savings and private property, a balanced social security, and the prohibition of the abuse of both political and economic power

- *Change and flexibility*—Implying the competition of people, ideas, products, and companies; a permanent need to adapt to constantly changing circumstances, both domestic and foreign; the need to be attentive not only to one's own needs and desires, but first of all to what others in the market need and require; the absence of permanently acquired market positions that are no longer economically viable.

Initially, the expression "social market economy" (*die soziale Marktwirtschaft*) was used to describe the reforms and policies adopted by the Federal

Republic of Germany following the currency reform of 1948. Although Germany was the most articulate and successful example, the basic concepts of the social market economy also have been present in the economic policies of most of the Western European countries. Although originally the basic concept, and the policies it implied, were subject to political controversies, by today they have become the common bases for economic policies throughout Western Europe.

The concept of the social market economy is of more than historic interest. It describes not only the reforms and policies adopted in the late 1940s and 1950s, but also the fundamental orientation of modern economic policies in Western Europe. If democracy and federalism are among the main features of the new, postwar political tradition of Western Europe, the social market economy represents the mainstream or the new European tradition in the area of economic policies. The social market economy is the expression of the belief that economic freedom is an essential part of political freedom. The relevance of the concept for Hungary is confirmed by the fact that important elements of the social market economy can be identified not only in the economic programs of various opposition groups, but also in significant portions of the latest version of the reform program of the current Hungarian government.

This report concludes that the concept of the social market economy is best suited for the successful economic and social transformation, modernization, and long-term growth of the Hungarian economy and for its integration into Europe and the world economy.

RELEVANT ASPECTS OF THE "SOCIAL MARKET ECONOMY"

In contrast to Keynesian economics, orthodox monetarism, or Marxism, the concept of the social market economy does not lend itself to textbook definitions. While it has a strong theoretical foundation, its important empirical dimension also must be emphasized.

■ Basic Concepts and Objectives

The basic objective of the social market economy is to promote economic efficiency through economic freedom and autonomy, through free exercise of the right to produce and consume within or outside the national borders. Economic freedom, however, does not imply the right to abuse freedom or to exercise economic power at the expense of society as a whole, of consumers, or of actual or potential competitors.

Successful social market economies require explicit, as well as implicit, rules of behavior. The respect for law and order in both private and public spheres is essential. Although both anecdotal evidence and statistics show differences in the degree of this "respect" (by the state and by the private sector) among the various countries concerned, the rule of law, as distinguished from the dominance of private interests or of political power, is the basis of the market economy.

A key objective of the social market economy is to promote economic prosperity on as wide a basis as possible, encompassing incomes, savings, and private property. This diffusion of prosperity is based primarily on eliminating discrimination and artificial obstacles to personal and private initiative and on creating the conditions of equal chances for equal effort and performance.

Solidarity, social cohesion (respectful of freedom), and social peace are among the fundamental features and objectives of the social market economy. Private or public "help for self-help" is an important aspect of the basic concepts discussed here. In that sense, fair market conditions, active social policies, and sectorial and/or regional policies (as well as measures in favor of small and medium-sized companies) are an integral part of the social market economy. They include active supervision and, if necessary, corrective measures in favor of the underprivileged and other victims of the market economy. Avoiding or reversing the pauperization of large or small segments of society is an essential dimension of the social market economy.

■ The Role of the State and of the Public Sector

The principal role of the state in this concept is to create and maintain the necessary framework and rules for the efficient and equitable working of the market economy (*conditions cadre* in French or *Rahmenbedingungen* in German).

State intervention (whether governmental or parliamentary) should conform to the market, i.e., it should promote the sound functioning of markets and avoid any serious erosion of the discipline and rationality of markets. Only where markets function inefficiently or in a way which causes serious harmful consequences should there be official interference. Where markets do not function fairly, however, the initiative for the necessary correction must not be left to the private sector alone.

The social market economy is not one of weak government but of limited government: "as much market as possible, and as much state as necessary."

Maintaining monetary stability to promote and protect the real value of private sector savings is among the key tasks of the public sector.

The protection and the careful management of public property is also one of the essential tasks of the state. This implies a careful and transparent management of public spending and receipts. Government, central and local, is responsible for the public good and not for the defense of the privileges of private groups or individuals.

Creating the basis for effective competition is an urgent task. Controlling excessive concentrations of economic power and promoting small and medium-sized companies are among the tasks of the state, as is providing the basic infrastructure and protecting the environment. The fulfilment of these tasks, however, must not lead to irrational or anti-economic policies (e.g., large prestige projects in the name of promoting infrastructure or breaking up companies under the ideology of smallness).

The behavior of the state in a social market economy is characterized by a balanced approach to the use of economic policy instruments: avoid extreme monetarism while neglecting fiscal policy; avoid extreme fiscal rigor, monetary laxness, financial speculation.

Finally, one of the main tasks of government is not only to create the conditions allowing the efficient functioning of markets, but also to help assure the social and political acceptance of the market economy.

CURRENT WESTERN EUROPEAN EXPERIENCE: A "BALANCED GROWTH POLICY"

Economic growth in Hungary has decelerated sharply in the past 10 years. It is an economic, social, and political imperative to reverse this trend. Without sustained and balanced economic growth, neither domestic nor external equilibrium can be achieved.

Some tend to fear today that the lack of growth during the 1980s has weakened the country's potential for growth during the 1990s. This study does not share this pessimism. If the appropriate microeconomic and macroeconomic policies are adopted, and with sufficient political and economic stability, the chances are good that Hungary will achieve sustained and balanced growth, with a corresponding increase in living standards, during the 1990s.

The chances for Hungarian economic growth can be illustrated by the experience of the Western European countries, which through the 1970s and the first half of the 1980s had experienced a similar loss of momentum. They, too, seemed about to succumb to "Europessimism," the belief in a permanently reduced rate of growth in Western Europe.

Today, "Europessimism" belongs to the past. European economies have been growing at a satisfactory rate for several years, and business, labor, and government are again confident about the medium and long-term outlook for European economies. Several factors were responsible for this remarkable improvement. Favorable external developments have played a role. But the principal credit belongs to the convergence of balanced macroeconomic and structural or microeconomic policies throughout Western Europe.

The last 10 years have witnessed a redefinition of the role of government in the economy, reducing its weight while increasing the efficiency of its action. Equally important has been the reduction of barriers to the free initiative of individuals and companies—a greater willingness to take risks, and greater opportunities to enjoy the benefits of economic success and performance.

The principle that "efficiency begins at home" has been widely recognized. Nevertheless, companies, regions, and countries have benefitted from the general improvement in the European economic environment.

One of the main fallacies of traditional "development economics" was the assumption that radically different economic policies have to be followed according to the level of income in various countries. Thus, even on the assumption that Hungary needs much more severe structural adjustments in the 1990s than the OECD countries needed in the 1970s and 1980s, the policies that have allowed Western Europe to grow again are still relevant for Hungary. These policies include:

- A balanced policy approach and a certain gradualism in macroeconomic and microeconomic measures gradually

- Long-term determination to fight inflation through checking both domestic and external sources

- Gradual, but determined approach to reducing budget deficits and excessive taxation levels. (The task of cutting back subsidies, transfer payments, and excessive corporate and personal taxes was carried out over a number of years, and is still not completed.)

- Closer control on public spending and, in particular, the elimination of prestige projects of dubious economic value

- Tighter management of public enterprises and policies to transfer them gradually to the private sector, to make them more profit conscious, profitable, and responsive to their customers

- Relatively tight monetary policies (without an exclusive reliance on orthodox monetarism) to restore the price function of interest rates for both savers and borrowers

- Attempts at deregulation and debureaucratization to facilitate innovation and business

- Policies favorable to exports, while avoiding competitive devaluations

- Policies to stabilize exchange rates with the help of the European Monetary System

- Active sectorial policies (in industry, agriculture, and the service sector), which imply an extensive participation of national, regional, and local government (as well as the European Community) in restructuring and gradually eliminating excess capacity and inefficient sectors and companies

- Active labor market policy, involving retraining, tax incentives, etc., to increase labor mobility and to ease the social burden of redundancies without massive transfer payments

- Policies to promote labor peace to reduce strikes and the often excessive wage settlements and to introduce modern labor-saving management and production techniques

- Active technology policy to promote research and development and the diffusion and valorization of modern and new technologies

- Announcement of the creation of a true internal market in Europe by the end of 1992, aimed at stimulating competition and increased efficiency through deepening and consolidating the achievements of 40 years of European and world-wide economic integration.

 ## A Joint Task Force of Officials from Hungary and the OECD Countries to Promote Hungary's Integration into the World Economy

The integration of Hungary and of the other Eastern European countries in the European and world economies has an important multilateral dimension through existing and future organizations (e.g., BERD). At the same time, the actual and potential actions of the multilateral organizations, and the numerous bilateral programs and measures currently being envisaged, have to be brought more sharply into focus and linked to the actual needs of Hungary and its progress toward a market economy. This is the objective of "Task Force Hungary," proposed in this section.

INTERNATIONAL COOPERATION AND THE HUNGARIAN ECONOMY'S CHANCES OF SUCCESS

Hungary has a chance to deal successfully with both the short-term economic situation and the longer term task of thoroughly transforming its economic structures. Private initiative, domestic and foreign, has a crucial role to play in this context. At the official level, coherent and efficient policies within Hungary and an organized approach to international cooperation are needed.

Concurrent with rapid domestic institutional innovation, it is also necessary to establish as soon as possible, a temporary, full-time group of Hungarian and Western officials to organize cooperation between Hungary and the OECD countries. Task force members should come from both national administrations and international organizations.

This task force must not become a new bureaucracy, nor should it revise earlier political decisions regarding cooperation with Eastern Europe. It should focus the efforts of the OECD countries to Hungary's greatest benefits.

The principal short-term objective of the cooperation and assistance offered by the OECD countries is to help prevent the threat of a breakdown of financial, economic, and social structures in Hungary and to plan the transition to an efficient market economy. The medium and long-term objective is to help promote economic growth through the successful transformation of the Hungarian economic system and through its effective integration into the European and world economy.

The economic and political success of the postwar European Recovery Program was as much due to its organizational quality and systematic policy coordination as to the generosity of the United States.

By now, most observers recognize that one of the major shortcomings of the heavy Western financing of East-West trade (including establishing turn-key plants) in the 1970s was the refusal, or the inability, of the West to insist on systemic adaptations or guarantees that would have enabled the borrowing countries to turn the loans to more productive uses and to repay their debts.

The negative experience of the 1970s and the current opportunities for much more political and economic changes than could be hoped for until very recently should provide the basis for a more systematic, more global, and more rational approach to organizing financial and technical assistance to, and cooperation with, Hungary and the other Eastern European countries. The rapid and extensive action undertaken in favor of East Germany by the Federal Republic, as well as by the rest of the Western community of nations, confirms the need for a well-planned action for the reconstruction and integration of the other Eastern European countries as well.

■ Cooperation and "Help for Self-Help"

It is clear that the principal objective of external assistance has to be "help for self-help." The success of the Hungarian economy depends primarily on Hungary and its people. This is the main lesson from both successful and unsuccessful examples of foreign assistance, in Europe and in the rest of the world, since the end of the Second World War.

Ultimately, economic success or the lack of it will be determined by the Hungarians themselves, by their ability and willingness to achieve both microeconomic and macroeconomic changes. However, the approach they adopt, the "models" they follow, will play a crucial role in determining whether they succeed or whether the Hungarian case will become a major missed opportunity also for the West.

Success will also depend on the quality of Western political and economic leadership and the ability of national and international administrations to organize their common effort effectively. The need for extensive technical assistance and for technology transfer in the broadest sense from the OECD countries has been recognized by both sides. This transfer of know-how and experience can and should take multiple forms (from joint ventures and other forms of direct investments to training courses organized by both private groups and government officials).

In addition, however, technical assistance on a more global level may prove to be indispensable. This should involve not only macroeconomic policy in the narrow sense, but also issues like banking and financial reform and policies, industrial and agricultural policies, the protection of the environment, privatization, and competition policy, among others.

Today there is no shortage of qualified economists in Hungary. Many of them are familiar with Western theories and developments. Many have a realistic view of the country's problems. There is, however, a lack of effective experience in dealing with the priorities and the day-to-day workings of a market economy, not only at the enterprise level, but especially at the governmental level.

The goal is to provide inspiration, not to impose any set of objectives or policies on Hungary. The independence of Hungary and of Hungarian policy-making will be important for domestic credibility and broad political support. The extent and continuation of Western assistance, however, will also be influenced by Hungarian achievements.

The objective is to help and to advise, and in some cases to warn about the consequences of certain policies or lack of policies. Hungarian policy makers must learn that economic policy making is as difficult in a market economy as in a Socialist economy.

This global technical cooperation (primarily at the level of public officials) should also reflect the pluralistic tradition of the OECD countries. However, it should not be organized on a purely *ad hoc* basis. An *ad hoc* approach would not allow non-Hungarian officials to become sufficiently familiar with the Hungarian situation. Ultimately, it may also be considered more as interference than as a situation in which Hungarian officials could have regular and systematic access to Western administrative and policy expertise.

In the short run when the most crucial decisions have to be made, this cooperation cannot (yet) take the form of full or even associate Hungarian membership in the major Western economic organizations (European Community, EFTA, or even the OECD). Moreover, even membership in these organizations would not necessarily provide the advice and expertise likely to be needed by the Hungarians in the period of transition. The more universal organizations (IMF and the World Bank) are used to provide global economic advice. Together with the Bank for International Settlements (BIS), they also have a useful role to play in Hungary. However, in terms of the effective transformation and international integration of Hungary, the resources of the OECD, the European Economic Community, and EFTA, on the one hand, and of the individual OECD countries, on the other hand, are the most relevant. Task Force Hungary would fill the urgent need to coordinate these resources and activities effectively.

The OECD countries are providing or planning to provide extensive help. This assistance should have the maximum positive impact both now and in the future. Historic experience shows that the outcome will depend not only on the quantity of the assistance, but also on its quality, and in particular on the quality of policy advice and mutual commitments.

However, despite the good will and the wealth of experience and resources, without a systematic and effective organization of the assistance and cooperation, the risks of waste and of failure remain considerable.

THE NEED FOR A TASK FORCE FOR HUNGARY

The full integration of Hungary into the international economy can only be accomplished gradually. It will require both domestic changes and a revision of the country's international economic relations. This process can be facilitated through systematic cooperation between Hungary and its foreign partners.

The speed and intensity of the political commitment and potential financial, administrative, and institutional involvement of the OECD countries (individually and collectively) and of various international organizations in supporting the current efforts in Eastern European countries are remarkable. Ultimately, public and private initiatives taken together could reach or exceed the dimensions of the postwar European Recovery Program, even if it is inappropriate to speak of a "New Marshall Plan."

Besides freeing substantial financial resources and providing easier access to OECD markets for the exports of Eastern European countries, Hungary's foreign partners show a willingness to intensify economic cooperation and advise and assist in areas ranging from macroeconomic policies to specific fields concerning the environment, training programs, quality controls, and financial markets, among others. This willingness is already obvious among the OECD countries and in the European Community, the IMF, and the World Bank. The work of the "Group of 24" and the agreement about a Bank for European Reconstruction and Development witness this development.

Nevertheless, under current institutional conditions, the dispersion of efforts is still a danger in Hungary and the other Eastern European countries, as well as among their international partners. This could lead to the waste of scarce material and human resources, as well as to contradictory or inappropriate advice and planning in the areas of structural changes, stabilization, and economic policy.

Some actions by their nature are and ought to remain bilateral or confined to existing, specialized organizations. Others, however, require a more concerted and systematic approach, as well as a certain institutional innovation, to obtain the expected results. The areas where concerted cooperation is required include both domestic and international tasks and challenges. Among the most evident tasks of coordination, consultation, and cooperation are the identification of the specific needs of Hungary and the survey of available resources and expertise among its foreign partners.

An equally important area is the coordination and provision of advice and planning related to the various aspects of macroeconomic and micro-economic reform and stabilization. In this crucial field the need is evident to use the expertise of organizations like the IMF, the World Bank, and the BIS, as well as the OECD and the various bodies of the European Community. However, international effort and technical assistance cannot be, and are not, limited to these organizations. In view of the novelty and magnitude of the task, the current operating practices and resources of these organizations (and the current degree of coordination among them) must be expanded to design the economic reforms needed in Hungary and the other Eastern European countries.

A related task is the coordination of the technical assistance and transfer of information and experience about the administrative problems and experience of various OECD countries. Hungarian officials and civil servants have to learn as much or more from their national counterparts than from experts of international organizations about the responsibilities and the day-to-day working of government in a market economy. The need for national officials in the OECD countries to learn and to know about the problems of the Hungarian economy belongs to the same category of challenges. Finally, a general forum (and assistance) is needed for consultations and negotiations between Hungary and other countries.

One of the principal conclusions and recommendations of this study is that the need for a concentrated effort to organize the cooperation between Hungary and the OECD countries aimed at creating the basis for the gradual and orderly integration of Hungary into the international economy cannot be fulfilled directly through existing institutions. The solution suggested here, Task Force Hungary, is not aimed at replacing or duplicating the existing national and international efforts, but rather to make them more effective and more directly operational. The work of this task force should be closely integrated into the general OECD effort in Eastern Europe (including East Germany). Thus, to work effectively toward these goals and to avoid a waste of effort on both sides, a mixed task force with a medium-term assignment, dedicated to the specific problems of Hungary and to facilitating the process of its transformation and international integration should be created at the earliest possible date.

THE OBJECTIVES AND SCOPE OF "TASK FORCE HUNGARY"

■ Objectives

The objective of Task Force Hungary would be to provide, during the crucial transition period, a common instrument for coordination, information, and if necessary, negotiation related to the cooperation between Hungary and the OECD countries. It will help to form the foundation for the effective integration of Hungary into the world economy.

No new permanent organization or bureaucracy should be created. Task Force Hungary should be dissolved after a period specified in advance. Task Force Hungary should reenforce the effectiveness of existing multilateral or national initiatives or actions within existing international organizations, rather than replace them. It should help coordinate, not centralize, all the multiple efforts aimed at furthering the international economic integration of Hungary.

Such a task force, however, would not only provide the necessary high visibility for the common effort, it would also help prevent a dispersion of efforts and allow a rational use of the limited resources of highly qualified people.

Finally, it would provide an excellent training ground not only for Hungarian officials, but also for nationals of OECD countries about conditions in Hungary.

In its concept and methods of work, it could be inspired by the original OEEC, which made a major contribution to the reconstruction and international liberalization and integration of the European countries in the 1950s.

■ Scope and Specific Tasks

1. Identify needs, problems and resources, and coordinate cooperation and actions to the benefit of the Hungarian economy.

2. Cooperate with other organizations engaged in actions related to Eastern Europe.

3. Provide a forum for consultation, obstacle identification, priority definitions, negotiations, or arbitrage.

4. Consider questions related to economic liberalization in various areas and move to eradicate obstacles to the development of Hungarian foreign trade.

5. Coordinate advice and assistance related to economic reforms and to the conduct of economic policy.

6. Consider issues related to direct investments and technology transfer.

7. Consider specific areas such as privatization, infrastructure, industrial policy, the environment, education, labor market, and social security, among others.

8. Facilitate technical assistance and information in the fields of public administration, central banking, and financial development, among others.

9. Assist in organizing information about Hungary and the flow of economic, business, and technical information toward Hungary.

10. Participate in the prevention of a breakdown of Eastern European trade and in achieving multilateral trade and convertibility with the other Eastern European countries and the Soviet Union.

Task Force Hungary ought to play a role in implementing the other recommendations presented in this chapter, in particular the creation of the Hungarian-International Long-Term Credit and Development Bank and technical assistance in the monetary and financial reforms described under the heading "Controlling Inflation . . ." in this chapter.

ORGANIZATION

■ Basic Concept

Task Force Hungary should work in close cooperation with the Hungarian and OECD governments and with various relevant international organizations, and should be integrated in the overall effort in Eastern Europe. Task Force Hungary should be a temporary organization of, for example, three years, with a strong practical orientation. It should consist of a small full-time staff, a certain number of officials and experts on temporary assignment, and working groups.

It should be headed by a General Secretary, who ought to be a European personality with strong public sector and business experience. Beside a Council, Task Force Hungary also ought to have a mixed Banking and Corporate Advisory Group.

The budget of Task Force Hungary should be jointly financed by the OECD countries and Hungary. The headquarters should be in Budapest.

■ Staff

The Secretariat and the officials and experts on temporary assignment ought to be recruited from among

- High-level officials from various OECD countries (central and local government, central banks)

- The business and banking communities

- Hungarian officials

- International civil servants (European Community Commission, EFTA, IBRD, IMF, BIS, OECD).

■ Working Groups
The working groups could include officials from various OECD countries, Hungarian officials, officials from other Eastern European countries, financial and business experts from these areas, experts from international organizations, and Hungarian businesspeople, managers, bankers, and labor representatives. The selection of the members of the Secretariat and of the working groups should be made, without bureaucratic in-fighting, on the basis of the effective needs of Hungary and the relevance of their experience for its economy.

3 A Hungarian-International Long-Term Credit and Development Bank for an Optimum Utilization of Resource Transfer

During the crucial early years of transformation from a Socialist economy into a market economy, Hungary, like the other Eastern European economies, will require a net inflow of resources. As far as possible, this inflow should not lead to a further accumulation of external debt. During the next three to five years, several avenues will have to be used simultaneously:

- Grants—as the Western European countries (including West Germany) received on a large scale following the Second World War

- Direct investments—not for balance-of-payments reasons, but to modernize the economy, transfer technology in the widest sense of the word, and integrate Hungarian companies into world markets

- Loans from governments and banks—probably on a more limited scale than that suggested by the credit offers reported in the daily press

- A negotiated debt-adjustment program—considering the long-term interests of both Hungary and the creditors, and including at least a temporary reduction in interest payments.

If no such inflow occurs, and Hungary's net interest payments remain near to current levels (or would have to rise as a result of further debt accumulation and of higher international interest rate levels) during the next three to five years, the chances of success of economic and social transformation would be seriously jeopardized. Ultimately this would lead to default on the country's outstanding debt.

To have the desired positive effect, this transfer will have to be more carefully, jointly managed than had been the case in the past. Since the capacity to service external financial obligations will be constrained by future earnings in foreign currencies, it is necessary to optimize the use of foreign borrowing and investment. Both in Hungary and abroad, a liberal, but orderly approach is required to capital imports. An excessive inflow of speculative capital (in particular in real estate, but also to purchase Hungarian companies) could induce capital flight from Hungary and lead to a political backlash.

The bank proposed in the present report should be one of the involvements of this more efficient management. The creation of this bank would be linked to the reform of the Hungarian National Bank and to the consolidation of the Hungarian banking and financial system discussed in the last section of this chapter.

This bank would not be in conflict, but would usefully complement the creation of the Bank for European Reconstruction and Development. Also, the objective of the bank is not to increase the volume of resources available to Hungary under the present institutional arrangements, but to assure that the best use is made of them.

THE NEED FOR A MORE EFFICIENT APPROACH FOR RESOURCE ALLOCATION AND TRANSFER

One of the urgent needs in Hungary is to create the institutional basis for a rational allocation of long-term investment funds. This task covers both productive and infrastructure investments.

The current problems and structural weaknesses of the Hungarian economy can be traced in part to inefficient allocation of financial resources in the past. This is particularly true of the use made of the funds borrowed abroad, especially in the 1970s and mid-1980s, and for some large, partly politically motivated, investment projects until the recent past. The principal short- and medium-term danger for Hungary is not the potential lack of external financial resources, but their uneconomical use.

Capital imports ought to help create the basis for sustained economic growth. However, as in the past in Hungary, and as is often the case with other capital-importing countries, "waste" of foreign resources can result from a lack or deficiency of market mechanisms at the microeconomic level, as well as of inappropriate macroeconomic policies. Thus, excessive external borrowing could be counterproductive. Misapplied, funds can finance new prestige projects, slow down internal adjustment, and even discourage or hamper domestic savings, thus adding to future balance-of-payment problems. An excessive inflow of private speculative capital, under the disguise of direct investments, should also be a source of concern.

Both Hungary and its foreign partners will benefit from preventing an inflationary leakage of new resource transfer into public or private consumption or into investments with a low rate of return (or even into capital exports or capital flight). At present, project finance has been emphasized to deal with the microeconomic risks of capital imports. Yet current conditions allow considerable scope for overlending or overborrowing and for financing projects that ought to have relatively low priority. Moreover, microeconomic risk is linked to macroeconomic policies. If capital imports lead to general financial laxness and subsequently to renewed balance-of-payment problems, repaying loans on appropriate projects will be more difficult, as well.

The lessons from the past and the analysis of the current situation show some major structural shortcomings of the decision process and of the management of lending and of resource transfer to Hungary and to other heavily indebted countries. The institutional mechanism for managing international lending to Hungary and other debtor countries has two aspects:

- Hungary's commitment (as of other countries in balance-of-payments difficulties) to follow good debtor policies, essentially defined in terms of fiscal and monetary austerity

- The green light, for Hungary and for potential official and private creditors, for an uncoordinated and a virtually indiscriminate expansion of short and long-term lending.

This type of institutional arrangement, as the experience of many countries has shown, carries two dangers:

- A substantial and fairly rapid further rise in Hungary's foreign debt

- Concurrently, no sufficient increase in Hungary's economic capacity to service its foreign debt.

A repetition of stop-go economic policies and of external payments and debt crises looms ahead unless both Hungary and its creditors change radically the management of the resource transfer to Hungary.

THE NEED FOR A NEW LONG-TERM CREDIT AND DEVELOPMENT BANK

Thus, one of the priority tasks for the Hungarian authorities and for Hungary's foreign partners ought to be the creation of a Hungarian-International Long-Term Credit and Development Bank with broad tasks and responsibilities. This bank, which ought to be set up as soon as possible, should be associated with the new Bank for European Reconstruction and Development. Its objectives, operations, and management ought to be focused on the Hungarian economy and include areas outside the scope of BERD. It should be located in Budapest (as, incidentally, could have been the case also for the BERD).

There are several important arguments for the creation of such a Hungarian long-term credit bank in addition to the BERD, with which it ought to cooperate very closely. It should be stressed that the bank is not proposed to obtain more public or private financial transfers to Hungary than is possible under the present or planned arrangements. The objective is to increase the effectiveness of these transfers.

The essential task of putting the long-term financing of productive investments and infrastructure on a sound basis in Hungary requires a systematic effort. A new specialized institution directly dedicated to Hungarian economic problems and becoming part of the Hungarian economy can make a major contribution to the solution of this problem. In view of the country's institutional and economic needs, the proposed bank would have a much broader scope and would have to play a much more direct role in the Hungarian economy than could be the case for the BERD.

Thus, in addition to specializing in project finance, the new bank would also help achieve and maintain domestic and external macroeconomic equilibrium through its role as a "Hungarian counterpart fund". Whereas the essential responsibility of the central bank ought to be monetary policy and the maintaining domestic and external stability, it would be the task of the new bank to assist the private and public sectors in the long-term development and modernization of the economy. In the reorganization of the Hungarian economy, the concept of the State Development Institute, responsible for financing large investment projects, will have to be completely revised. Besides its key role in the sound management of external resource transfer, the bank would also help to raise banking and financial standards in Hungary.

THE OBJECTIVES AND PRINCIPAL TASKS OF THE BANK

The models and precedents for the suggested bank include the German Reconstruction credit bank (Kreditanstalt für Wiederaufbau) or the long-term credit banks in Japan in the early decades of their activity. It is understood, however, that the exact scope of the responsibilities and tasks of the bank should be defined according to the needs and conditions of the Hungarian economy. The bank's functions and the scope of its responsibilities, as well as its capital structure, would most likely change over time. The original concept for the bank would be maintained only as long as the private sector cannot effectively fulfill the same functions, and as long as a counterpart fund is needed.

■ General Tasks and Operating Rules

The bank would be independent. Its main task and responsibility would be the efficient management of the foreign transfer of resources to Hungary in view of improving the country's international competitive position and increasing its productive capacity.

The bank would cooperate closely with the Hungarian National Bank, the government, and commercial banks, as well as with international financial organizations, foreign banks, and governments. It would also assume the role of a counterpart fund for resource transfer. The credit bank would be an important instrument in separating the control of the long-term external financing of Hungarian development and modernization both from the current activity of the National Bank and from the government budget. The Bank could assume a leading role in the transactions or in some cases provide only technical expertise and supervision.

■ Microeconomic and Development Tasks

Among the specific microeconomic tasks, promoting the creation and the development of internationally competitive Hungarian private enterprises (especially small- and medium-sized companies) would be the first priority. The bank would also emphasize the promotion of export-oriented companies in industry, agriculture, tourism, and other services. The bank could provide assistance (financial and technical) in direct investment operations in Hungary.

The bank would also participate in restructuring and consolidating existing companies, especially when foreign partners are involved. Parallel with the consolidation of companies, the bank could participate in restructuring and consolidating banks, the financial sector, and markets.

As mentioned above, the bank would cooperate closely with other Hungarian banks and financial institutions. In carrying out its tasks, the bank would have to avoid specializing in low-risk credits at the expense of the rest of the banking system. It would have to seek a healthy balance between ordinary financing and industrial/financial innovation over time.

■ Infrastructure

One of the major tasks of the bank would be to promote infrastructure projects, with a priority on what might be called "productive infrastructure" projects. It would have to assume some of the tasks of the State Development Institute. Besides the financing aspect, there is also a need for considerable improvement in infrastructure planning in Hungary. The examples of the Bös-Nagymaros project and of the handling of the planned Vienna-Budapest World Exhibition illustrate the need for a review of the existing system and for identifying long-term needs and priorities.

■ Environment

Another priority task of the bank would be to participate in financing projects related to the protection of the environment.

■ Macroeconomic Tasks

The new bank, the National Bank, and the Hungarian government (specifically, the Ministry of Economics and Finance) will need to cooperate closely and maintain an effective division of labor. Through its policies and its authority the bank would be able to exert a positive influence with respect to the macroeconomic impact of the resource transfer from abroad.

The bank would play an active role in the management of the Hungarian external debt and in avoiding excessive borrowing from abroad, as well as in limiting the potential inflationary impact of capital imports. This could involve, for example, freezing the forint counterpart of external resource transfers (e.g., grants, some of the official borrowing and proceeds from the sale of assets to foreign investors). It could also involve transforming domestic savings via savings instruments such as marketable investment funds, convertible bonds, equity issues, and the like. While the bank would concentrate on medium- and long-term operations, it could be also attentive to short-term credit developments.

The bank would be in a position to counteract the frequent occurrence of long-term tied loans (often appearing as project finance) and the open or disguised use of long-term borrowing for balance-of-payment purposes.

Lastly, the bank would also have to be instrumental in consolidating the balance sheet of the National Bank and retiring the government's long-term debt.

STRUCTURE OF THE BANK

The functions and operating procedures would have to be subject to periodic review.

■ Capital

The capital of the bank could be provided by OECD governments, Western creditor banks, the Hungarian Government, IBRD, and BERD. The OECD governments and the creditor banks would have a combined initial majority of the capital.

A gradual privatization of the bank should be planned over a specific period, for example, over the next 10 years. At the end of this period, Hungary should assume majority control of the capital of the Bank.

■ Control and Management

Policy control would be exercised by a board comprising governors or directors nominated by the Hungarian government, the Hungarian National Bank, the OECD governments, and the creditor banks. On certain specific issues, each of the four would have a qualified veto power. The bank would have to have an autonomous management, headed by a president or a managing director, who initially would be a highly qualified Western financial personality. This person would be seconded by a Hungarian deputy managing director and an active executive committee formed by the board.

The bank's Policy Advisory Committee would have to include representatives of the BERD, IMF, IBRD, Hungarian National Bank, and Hungarian banks and financial institutions. The Corporate Advisory Committee could include representatives of large and small companies from Hungary and various other countries.

The bank would be staffed by Hungarian and Western experts. These latter (some of whom could be on temporary assignment) would have to be recruited both from the private sector and from national administrations, as well as from the IBRD and the European Investment Bank (EIB).

RESOURCES OF THE BANK

The bulk of the resources of the bank, especially during an initial period of one to three years, would have to come from outside Hungary.

■ Public Sources

The public sources of the bank's resources would fall into the following categories:

- Long-term government credits, whether for project finance or without specific allocation

- Government grants or concessionary financing (e.g., in the framework of debt-relief operations, environmental protection projects, etc.)

- Credits from international organizations (IBRD, BERD).

■ Private Sources, International

The bank would have essentially three major private sources of funds at its disposal:

- The counterpart of the purchase of participations in Hungarian state-owned companies by foreign investors

- The counterpart of debt-relief operations by foreign creditor banks (interest reductions, reductions of principal)

- Long-term borrowing on the international capital markets.

■ Private Sources, Hungarian

At a later stage, the bank could also raise funds from individuals and from institutional investors on the capital market to be developed in Hungary.

PREREQUISITES TO THE REALIZATION AND SUCCESSFUL OPERATION OF THE CREDIT BANK

■ Prerequisites to Realization

The chances for the creation of such a bank appear good. In fact, the suggestion corresponds to the general thinking in Hungary and in the OECD countries at the official and private level.

The principal prerequisite for the creation of a credit bank is political. The OECD countries and Hungary have to realize that the bank would benefit both the Hungarian economy and foreign creditors and investors.

On the Western side, it is also important to see the proposed bank as the most appropriate and most pragmatic solution not only for the interaction among various interested organizations (such as the IMF, IBRD, and the new BERD), but also for coordinating the interests and the policies of public and private creditors. The fragmentation characteristic of the current situation could jeopardize the success of economic reform and the chances for sustained growth of the Hungarian economy.

On the Hungarian side, the single most important requirement for the creation of the bank is the determination to make the most effective use of scarce financial resources and, in particular, of various forms of capital imports and resource transfers. Hungary's leaders and the Hungarian people must be convinced of the advantages of close cooperation with Hungary's private and official creditors, which would become possible through the proposed bank. It has to be seen as an integral part of a global concept of development and of financial and monetary consolidation of the various sectors and institutions, including the reform of the Hungarian National Bank (cf. Section 5 on "Controlling Inflation..." in this chapter).

It also has to be realized that the credit bank would not limit competition either among foreign creditors or investors or among the potential users of resources in Hungary. In fact, one of its main purposes would be to facilitate the change from a politically negotiated distribution of financial resources in Hungary to a market-oriented distribution. A stipulation of "autoliquidation," privatization and transformation of its functions, after, for example, 10 years would underscore its contribution to the development of a healthy market economy. Hungarians must realize that its objective would not be to limit Hungarian sovereignty. The efficient joint management of the external resource transfers would provide a greater freedom of action for Hungarian authorities to adopt policies favorable to sustained and socially equitable growth and development than is the case today, when the country is faced with recurring short-term balance-of-payment crises, constant external pressures to follow stringent austerity policies, and the continued growth of its foreign debt.

■ **Prerequisites to Success**

Time is an important factor of success. Speed is required because planning for the bank must be coordinated with the structural reforms of the Hungarian economy and with the development of long-term economic policies. This is true in particular for the reform of the central bank and of the banking and financial sector, for the adjustment of Hungary's foreign debts, and for the development of an effective anti-inflationary program.

The creation of such a bank requires a concentrated economic and political effort. The relatively small group that will be in charge of the planning should include Hungarian experts and officials, representatives of Western governments and of the private banks, as well as experts from the relevant international organizations (IMF, IBRD, BIS, EIB, OECD). A recognized, independent international individual from the banking community ought to be entrusted with the coordination of this major planning effort.

The active cooperation of the proposed bank with the creditor banks, in strictly financial terms as well as at the management level and in establishing contacts with the international business community, would be of great importance, both for the success of the credit bank itself and for the development of the Hungarian economy as a whole.

The need for autonomy and for reliable and innovative management as the prerequisites for long-term success cannot be overemphasized.

CREATING A HUNGARIAN INTERNATIONAL LONG-TERM CREDIT AND DEVELOPMENT BANK WITH FUNCTIONS OF A DOMESTIC COUNTERPART FUND

Objective: Not to increase resource transfer to Hungary beyond what would be available under present arrangements, but to assure optimum use and contribution to Hungarian economic development.

To serve specific Hungarian needs. Inspiration from *Kreditanstalt Fuer Wiederaufbau* and Japanese long-term credit banks.

1. There is a widely recognized need for a more efficient approach for resource allocation and resource transfer.

2. The creation at the earliest possible date of a new Hungarian-International Long-Term Credit and Development Bank would be a major contribution.

3. OECD partners, governments and creditor banks, could have an oversight role and could assist Hungarians in this task.

4. The creation of the credit bank should coincide with completing reform of the Hungarian national bank and the banking and financial system.

5. The credit bank, located in Budapest and specializing in business related to Hungary, would work closely with new Bank for European Reconstruction and Development.

Control and Management

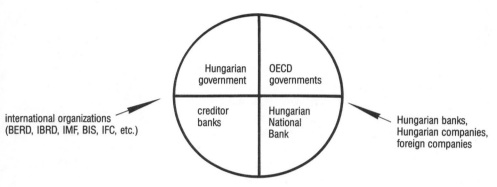

(with qualified veto powers, a temporary Western majority)

Headed by an outstanding
dynamic international financial personality

Macroeconomic Tasks

- Oversight of macroeconomic impact of resource transfer from abroad

- Participation in external debt management

- Sterilization of the forint counterpart of external resourcers

Selected Microeconomic and Development Tasks

- Promoting Hungarian private enterprises (small and medium-sized companies)

- Contribution to bank and corporate consolidation

- Productive infrastructure projects

- Environmental protection projects

4 A Negotiated Long-Term Debt Adjustment Program

A balanced and carefully negotiated debt-relief package will benefit not only the Hungarian economy, but also its creditors and the international financial community as a whole. Hungary's foreign debt occupies an important place in the debate on the prospects of the Hungarian economy. The convertible currency foreign debt has increased substantially in the 1980s. If a major financial crunch is to be avoided, the Hungarian government has to continue to borrow abroad, and a further increase in the debt is projected in the years to come.

Unlike other heavily indebted countries in Latin America or Poland in Eastern Europe, Hungary has made a consistent effort to meet its external financial obligations and to maintain good relations with its creditor banks. The Hungarian authorities have made it clear that they do not foresee taking initiatives for a Brady-Plan type debt relief package. This policy was confirmed during negotiations with the International Monetary Fund and by the austerity budget, the adoption of which the previous government pushed through Parliament in late December 1989.

Nevertheless, outside observers agree that a comprehensive debt-relief package is necessary if Hungary is to succeed in its attempt at domestic economic, political, and social reform and if sustained growth is to be achieved in the years ahead. Current debt management policies lead, on the one hand, to a continued rise of the country's foreign debt, and, on the other hand, through the excessive reliance on domestic austerity measures, to a weakening of Hungary's productive fabric and its long-term capacity to meet its external financial obligations.

THE HUNGARIAN DEBT PROBLEM

The current gross long-term debt of Hungary in convertible currencies is on the order of $20.5 billion; its gross external assets are $5 to $5.5 billion. Foreign debt grew rapidly during two periods, 1974 to 1979 and 1985 to 1987, when the net foreign debt increased by $5.9 billion (partly due to the appreciation of the German mark and the Japanese yen). Between 1982 and 1988, with the exception of the years 1984 to 1986, there was a large net external transfer from Hungary.

Over 85 percent of Hungary's long-term debt is owed to private creditors (mostly banks); about 30 percent of the total debt is owed to Japanese banks. The share of Japanese banks is of the order of 40 to 50 percent for medium- and long-term financial credits. The average maturity in 1987 was 9 years (8.5 to private creditors). The debt service in 1988 represented close to 45 percent of the export of goods and services. Currently, the annual debt service exceeds $2.5 billion, of which interest payments are in excess of $1 billion. Whereas in 1989 Hungary accumulated substantial transferable ruble assets (the current account surplus in nonconvertible currencies amounted to 1.6 billion rubles in 1989), the convertible debt was increased further by the $1.4 billion current account deficit (which, in contrast to 1988, exceeded net interest payments).

As a result of a net outflow to the IMF (suspension of the standby agreement in May 1989) and low disbursements by the World Bank, the share of commercial bank financing increased sharply in 1989. Official projections for 1990 suggest a net external borrowing requirement of $1.2 billion. Provided that the IMF standby agreement is renewed, lending from official sources could more than cover the net external borrowing, leading to a small net reduction of the debt to commercial banks.

As is the case for a number of other heavily indebted countries, the accumulation of a large external debt by Hungary and the heavy burden of servicing the debt result from a combination of internal policy errors and external developments.

The 1970s witnessed excessive borrowing to raise living standards and to compensate for the lack of structural adaptation to the changes taking place in the world economy following the first oil crisis. Imported capital was often channelled into consumption, ill-conceived prestige projects, or (indirectly) into financing ruble exports. According to the Hungarian National Bank, the share of capital inflows invested in export industries did not exceed 10 to 15 percent of the total. The sharp rise in the nominal and real rate of interest on the international capital markets (in contrast to the low or even negative rates prevailing in the 1970s) resulting initially from the determined anti-inflationary stance of the leading OECD countries following the second oil price crisis, and subsequently from the persistence of major imbalances in international payments also had a strong impact on Hungary. As for creditors, in line with the general practice of sovereign lending, they made little or no attempt to control the use of loans or to ascertain that capital imports would be put to good use in creating the productive resources to maintain interest payments and eventually retire the loans. This situation was not unique to the Eastern European countries. It reflected the general practice of the international banking community resulting from the recycling of petro dollars in the 1970s and early 1980s.

DEFUSING THE HUNGARIAN DEBT PROBLEM

Many view Hungary's external debt as a potentially explosive issue from a political, economic, and financial point of view for both Hungary and its Western partners. However, such an explosion is not inevitable, neither must the debt service be a permanent brake on Hungary's economic growth.

Management of the external debt must not remain the single most important determinant in Hungarian economic and social policies. The debt problem must not become the central issue in internal reform, nor in the relationship between Hungary and the OECD countries, nor in the integration of the Hungarian economy into the European and world economies. Making debt and the debt service the single most important variable of Hungarian economic policy would not in itself increase Hungary's ability to pay the interest charges and to repay the debt.

An orderly solution is possible, and Hungary, its creditor banks, and the OECD governments will benefit from cooperating in an orderly approach to defusing the debt problem. Debt adjustment should be linked with the creation of the Hungarian-International Long-Term Credit and Development Bank and with the consolidation and reform of the Hungarian National Bank.

The development of a Hungarian package must not be delayed until it is triggered (and its effectiveness diminished) by a financial or social crisis or by a unilateral moratorium or the partial repudiation of the external debt incurred by the former "Communist State." Any one of these developments would have severe negative economic and political consequences for Hungary, the OECD countries, and in particular for Western Europe. If *de facto* or *de jure* debt relief is postponed until a major internal crisis in Hungary forces unilateral action by the freely elected new Hungarian government, it would seriously discredit the ability and willingness of the OECD countries, and in particular of the European governments, to provide effective and efficient help for the transformation of the Eastern European economies. It would also be a major setback for the future development of market economies in Eastern Europe.

It is clear that the actual debt relief package can only be negotiated after the coming elections. It has to be closely linked to the domestic economic, social, and financial program of the new government, as well as to the realization of the other recommendations mentioned above, including the creation of the long-term credit bank and the organization of an effective Task Force Hungary.

Preliminary planning and coordination between the banks and the most directly interested Western governments ought to start immediately. The outline of a proposal, which could be the starting point of the negotiations, should have been ready for discussion with the new Hungarian government by Spring 1990.

PRINCIPLES AND MAIN FEATURES OF A HUNGARIAN DEBT ADJUSTMENT PROGRAM

■ Principal Objectives

The following ought to be the main objectives of the suggested debt-relief package for Hungary:

- Assist in creating the necessary conditions for sustained and balanced growth in the Hungarian economy and for its modernization and progress towards a dynamic market economy

- Facilitate the gradual integration of Hungary into the international economy

- Safeguard the legitimate interests of Hungary's creditors

- Avoid a situation in which the inflow of private speculative capital imports is tolerated, or even encouraged, to ease the pressure on the balance of payments

- Assist Hungary in clarifying the situation of its (nonliquid) external claims on other CMEA (Council of Mutual Economic Assistance) countries, as well as on certain developing countries, and help Hungary recover or make liquid some of these assets (the EPU experience is pertinent)

- Avoid unilateral action and a social or political crisis in Hungary and create the basis for continued good relations between Hungary and the international financial community.

■ Basic Principles of Debt Relief

The debt relief program ought to be conceived in a spirit of cooperation (as in the case of a private company having difficulty), based on the mutual interest of Hungary and its creditors to increase productive and earning capacity and to strengthen the financial position (and creditworthiness) of Hungary.

The approach to be adopted should take into account several basic principles. The program should aim at transforming the net outflow of resources from Hungary into a net flow of resources toward Hungary during the coming years. At the same time, to the extent possible, this flow of resources should not be debt creating. It should not lead to growth of the net external debt of the various relevant debt service ratios. Whereas debt/equity swaps may play a useful role within an overall plan, the need for a careful approach and the limits of what is possible in quantitative terms have to be recognized from the start both by Hungarians and by the international financial community.

An immediate objective should be to reduce, at least temporarily, the weight of interest payments. It is also necessary to lengthen the maturity of Hungary's outstanding debt.

The debt adjustment program ought to include a timetable and be oriented toward achieving certain specific microeconomic goals, such as the furthering of private enterprise, the promotion of small and medium-sized companies, and the realization of infrastructure projects, as well as the protection of the environment.

A system of guarantees for interest payments combined with interest reductions (similar to the mechanism suggested in late 1989 in the report of a high-level Expert Group for the Swiss government on the international debt problem) should be developed with the participation of Hungary, the creditor banks, and the governments of OECD countries. This guarantee system should depend on a system of indicators of the performance of the Hungarian economy and of general conditions in the world economy. As is the case with shares in a company, debt service payments could be linked to market conditions and the country's ability to pay.

Equitable burden-sharing among the banks, the Western governments, and Hungary, on the one hand, will avoid the impression that Hungarian banks are being bailed out and, on the other hand, will provide official guarantees or concessionary finance for interest-rate reduction and guarantee.

As mentioned above, the debt adjustment program should be closely coordinated with the creation of the Hungarian-International Long-Term Credit and Development Bank, the reform of the National Bank, and the development of a credible long-term economic program by the Hungarian government. The program should also provide for close monitoring (partly via the proposed new long-term credit bank) of the macroeconomic and the microeconomic use of the forint counterpart of the debt relief.

One of the objectives and tools of the program should be the promotion of foreign direct investments in Hungary by, for example, transforming outstanding debt into direct (equity) investment (e.g., through debt/equity swaps). The close cooperation of the creditor banks with Hungarian and foreign officials should help avoid abuses and psychological or policy errors in this context (no *Ausverkauf der Heimat*). The banks could be involved in the consolidation and restructuring of Hungarian companies. The close involvement of international banks and international companies is likely to have an overall positive impact and could help reduce the danger of capital flight.

Finally, as mentioned above, careful planning and rapid progress are essential from the point of view of both the creditor banks and of the future success of the Hungarian economic program.

■ Organization of Debt Relief

Several aspects of the organization of the debt adjustment program should be mentioned:

- Initial planning, as mentioned above, by the creditor banks and selected OECD governments

- Triangular planning and negotiation involving the Hungarian authorities, selected OECD Governments, and the creditor banks. (The international financial organizations, IMF, IBRD, and BIS, would be expected to provide their assistance to the three sides during the planning and negotiations.)

- Close coordination of the debt relief program with the medium- and long-term economic reforms being planned and realized in Hungary

- Close coordination of the debt relief program with other resource transfers and capital import programs in Hungary

- Parallel actions and negotiations, with the assistance of the creditor banks, involving Hungary's nonliquid external assets.

Changes in Hungarian
Medium-Term Convertible Currency Debt, 1981–1988
($US Million)

	1981	1982	1983	1984	1985	1986	1987	1988
Borrowing	1,443	1,389	1,628	3,079	4,014	3,802	3,108	2,324
Repayment	− 826	− 894	− 1,216	− 1,681	− 2,209	− 2,650	− 2,286	− 2,141
Net Interest Payments	− 1,102	− 970	− 662	− 744	− 725	− 829	− 924	− 1,048
Borrowing by Category:								
World Bank	—	—	18	121	111	180	269	273
International Monetary Fund	—	235	352	436	—	—	—	220
Syndicated Loans	550	400	475	967	494	1,338	1,401	200
Bonds	—	—	—	42	971	457	553	775
Bank to Bank	663	494	483	1,342	2,015	1,638	665	431
Trade Related	230	260	300	171	423	189	230	425

Controlling Inflation, Promoting Private Property and Competition, and Completing the Reform of the National Bank

The fifth set of recommendations is closely linked with the implementation and success of the preceding four measures. They deal with domestic and external stability, effective competition, and the development of private property, which are all preconditions for sound and undistorted economic growth and for the integration of Hungary's economy into the European and world economy.

Following are the principal issues on which further action is needed:

- Control of inflation
- Competition, liberalization, and an effective wage and price policy
- Completion of the reform and consolidation of the monetary, banking, and financial system, and the creation of a truly autonomous central bank
- Promotion of savings, the development of private property, privatization, and foreign direct investments
- Exchange rate policy and increasing the scope for convertibility.

It is necessary to distinguish among three aspects of the monetary and banking sector:

- The basic structures, instruments, and rules required for the Hungarian economy
- The short- and medium-term changes required to create the system
- The monetary and financial policies to be followed to assure a balanced growth of the economy.

THE NEED TO CHECK INFLATION

The members of the advisory group to this study agreed unanimously about the need for increased and sustained attention to the problem of inflation in Hungary. It is one of the most important tasks of the new government to avoid a further acceleration of inflation, to reduce the rate of price increases, and to devise an effective long-term anti-inflationary program. No responsible Hungarian decision makers should listen to domestic or external advice which takes lightly the problem of inflation.

The current inflation in Hungary is in no way comparable to the situation in Poland, Yugoslavia, or Argentina. Nevertheless, double-digit inflation for several years is and ought to be a source of concern, notwithstanding the claim that some of its initial causes are the elimination of unrealistic price structures and the avowed objective of bringing Hungarian prices more in line with world prices. Inflation at this rate creates new distortions which may be as difficult to cope with as the old ones. Also, at this level, inflation becomes more difficult to keep within bounds, and the economic and social costs of anti-inflationary policies tend to increase. There is less room for policy errors, and at least a hypothetical danger of slipping into a strong cumulative inflationary spiral and hyperinflation.

Hungarians know that slipping into hyperinflation must be avoided. Hyperinflation destroys indiscriminately both money savings and productive assets throughout the economy. The destructive impact of hyperinflation is felt throughout the productive structure and social fabric of a country long after it has been temporarily or permanently controlled. Hyperinflation creates economic and social distortions, as well as negative individual and collective economic and social reflexes, which are incompatible with the orderly development of a modern economy. In fact, the international record shows very few successful economic reforms following hyperinflation.

Although there have been no signs of hyperinflation and no massive flight into goods or foreign currency, inflation continues to accelerate. It increased gradually in 1987 and 1988 to nearly 20 percent in 1989. Official forecasts for 1990 at the beginning of the year put the rate of growth for consumer prices at 20 percent, most of which was "built-in" through the increases of basic commodities and rents and the effects of the downward adjustment of the exchange rate. The principal source of economic and social hardships today is inflation. Pressure for anticipatory price and wage increases is growing throughout the economy.

Nevertheless, the previous government claimed that inflation is under control. They pointed to the fact that the Hungarian inflation rate, although higher than the present OECD norm and the Hungarian rate in the 1970s and 1980s, is comparable to the inflation rates of some of the OECD countries in the 1970s. They also hoped that the severe cutbacks of the public-sector deficit and rationing credit to the economy would help keep inflation under control in the future. A further measure announced in January 1990, aimed at containing inflationary demand and liquidity creation, was the temporary suspension of all export permits to the CMEA countries to stop the swelling of the ruble export surplus.

Inflation is a serious problem in Hungary today. Among the consequences and dangers connected with it, the following should be recalled. Inflation will hit hardest those who benefit the least from liberalization and will weaken the social acceptance of the market economy. Money loses its value very rapidly at this rate, which discourages savings and perpetuates an excess, speculative demand in the economy (e.g., a flight into goods). Because of the lack of confidence in the national currency, little or no progress can be expected toward convertibility. Inflation can be seen (and not without justification) as a means to perpetuate the economic privileges of those who were in power. The longer inflation lasts, and the more ingrained the inflationary mentality, the more painful stabilization will be and the more uncertain its chances of success. Finally, continued high inflation could seriously slow down and jeopardize Hungary's chances of integration with the European economies.

Subsidies must be reduced. The free formation of prices and the absence of price distortions are essential features of the market economy. The arbitrary setting of prices, as well as the temporary wage and price freezes, are usually ineffective and often lead to a subsequent wage and price explosion. Yet, double-digit inflation is harmful for the market economy and an especially dangerous basis on which to build a modern market economy.

In a mixed economy like that of Hungary—with considerable market imperfections, local and sectorial monopoly positions, often incomplete and inefficient fiscal and monetary policy instruments, and important leakages in the financial system—it may be too much to expect to be able to deal with the problem of inflation almost exclusively through macroeconomic policy. Nevertheless, although it would not be realistic to aim at zero inflation in the near future, it should be possible to introduce an appropriate package to reverse the current trend and gradually reduce inflation toward single digits within a reasonable time frame without seriously adverse economic, social, or political consequences.

In addition to an appropriate macroeconomic framework, microeconomic measures and the combination of the reform of the central bank and of the Hungarian banking and financial system are needed. Besides liberalization, the program will have to include a careful price and wage policy in the public sector and other areas where competition and market pressures have not become effective yet. Many market conform models exist in the OECD countries for such policies. Careful management of external resources and of the external resource transfer are essential to creating the basis for long-term domestic and external stability. This requirement includes the effective sterilization of the forint counterpart of some of the capital transfers (such as grants, official borrowing, or the sale of state-owned assets) and a more stringent and rational approach for the selection of major projects to be financed through external credits than that taken in the past.

The direction and goals have to be clearly set and defined from the outset. Timing is important and realistic intermediate goals have to be set to avoid creating false expectations and discrediting the policies and objectives.

■ Inflation and the Policy Measures of Late 1989

In view of their pronounced inflationary impact, the logic of recent economic policy decisions of November 1989 (which put the main burden of the necessary price, fiscal, and external adjustment on food prices, rents, and other housing costs and basic services) may be questioned. It remains to be seen whether these measures will help reduce the bloated bureaucracy and overstaffing in the productive sectors, increase flexibility in the economy, and provide incentive for greater effort in the crucial months ahead. There are fears that inflation will slow down productivity improvements and the provision of better services, and that lower subsidies will simply be passed on to the population in the form of higher prices and rents.

Actual and projected increases in the cost of living will further exacerbate the hardships and difficulties of the population and could delay the necessary labor shedding for reasons of social hardship (especially in the innumerable "administrative" positions), constituting a further brake on the mobility of labor. An increased cost of living may create considerable social tension and add to the wage-price spiral.

If the new government were forced to adopt a general wage-price freeze later in 1990 to master a situation getting out of hand, this would not solve the problem and would only prepare the ground for a new explosion at a later date.

For industrial prices, with the major exception of CMEA trade, Hungary has already achieved a more rational price structure than in the past. Economic rationality in food and housing prices and other basic services is also important, not only in the highly developed industrialized countries, but also in resource-poor countries that suffer from low productivity and a wasteful utilization of the available human, financial, and material resources. Nevertheless, it is important to remember that the record (in Europe and in the rest of the world) of structural reforms that started with "truth in food prices and rents," while neglecting other major sources of waste and distortions in the economy, besides the social costs, is not very positive in purely economic terms. Rising food prices and rent are not good places to tie up excess liquidity or to free resources for productive uses.

The current debate on the situation and policies to be followed in Eastern Europe frequently references the success of the 1948 German currency reform and price and economic liberalization. Thus, it may be useful to remember that the Adenauer-Erhard government chose a different approach to eliminate price distortions and to quicken the return to a market economy in Germany:

> The success of decontrol may fairly be regarded as a major piece of evidence in favor of the Marktwirtschaft doctrine. . . . The impression has sometimes been conveyed that the German policy consisted of the uniform application of a simple principle. This was by no means the case. The lifting of (price) controls was a bold step but not a blind one. It was limited to sectors of the economy where incentives were likely to have the greatest effect, where instability of prices could do relatively little damage, and where controls would have been the hardest to administer. It centered therefore upon manufactured consumer goods. . . . As it was, prices rose, but basic stability was maintained because labor did not press strongly for wage increases. This restraint would have been almost impossible if food prices and

rents had not been kept down. An all-round rise in living costs would probably have resulted in a price-wage spiral or in the reimposition of price controls. Either development would almost certainly have slowed down the recovery. All in all, therefore, the policy of selective decontrol seems to have achieved a fairly good balance between boldness and caution. The German experience demonstrates the effectiveness of free markets, but it does not speak against the use of controls where pressures are powerful. . . ." [Henry Wallich, *Mainsprings of the German Revival*, 1955, pp. 122–124]

■ Stabilization, Repressed Inflation, and Dealing with Monetary Overhang

In Hungary, as in many countries faced with fundamental structural changes and considerable uncertainty about the short- and long-term economic outlook, there is concern about an actual or potential monetary overhang. Such an overhang is a source of open or repressed inflation. It leads to or reinforces inefficient resource allocation. It is also an important obstacle to decontrolling prices and to external liberalization and convertibility.

The size of this overhang, however, is not fixed or given at any one moment in time. It depends on the relationship between the available liquid means of payments (money), on the volume of goods and services available in the economy, on the level of prices, and on people's confidence in the economic and monetary outlook (the velocity of money circulation). A loss of confidence in the currency and strong inflationary expectations can lead to an acceleration of the velocity of circulation and to a flight into goods or foreign currencies. This problem can be aggravated by a parallel cutback in the supply of goods available (i.e., retention of goods by the producers).

It is difficult to project the future velocity of circulation in case of a sudden loss of confidence. On the basis of the available evidence, however, it may be assumed that at present, in quantitative terms, the monetary overhang is not a major force in Hungary. It is certainly not comparable to that in Germany after the war, which led to the identification of the very problem of repressed inflation, nor of the recent situations in Poland or Yugoslavia. However, all Socialist countries have suffered to a smaller or greater extent from repressed inflation as a result of the distorted price structures and the governments' systematic deficit financing of civilian and military spending. In Hungary, its existence is illustrated by the pent-up demand for foreign goods by households and companies.

The following approaches, or any combination of them, may be used for dealing with the problem of monetary overhang:

- Allow prices to rise (open inflation) to absorb the excess liquidity

- Cut spending, and thereby the volume and speed of money entering the economy

- Improve conditions for savings and for holding liquid assets

- Absorb excess demand through increasing the supply of goods, taxation, or conversion into long-term assets

- Freeze or confiscate liquid holdings across the board

- Reduce the value of money.

The first four measures are routine in anti-inflationary policy. They are usually applied in combination, the emphasis on one or the other depending on the situation and on the economic and political preferences of the country concerned. The last two are much more radical. They are called for when the excess liquidity or the monetary overhang is too large to be dealt with through regular instruments. Like hyperinflation, they involve a massive confiscation of pent-up (and unfulfillable) purchasing power. To use Rueff's terminology, they imply a massive elimination of "false claims" or *faux droits*.

Whichever measures are to be used, and in whatever combination, they must build confidence in the credibility of policy and confidence in the future value of money and financial assets. As experience has shown time and again, without confidence, none of the technical measures (neither the more gradual ones, nor the massive monetary reforms) aimed at dealing with the problem of monetary overhang have ever had a lasting result.

In Hungary, the task of stabilization and dealing with the problem of repressed inflation and with an effective or potential monetary overhang ought to be manageable as a result of the ongoing liberalization of the economy.

Thus, on the basis of the statistics and other evidence available in Hungary, drastic monetary cuts—i.e., for the elimination or the confiscation of a significant portion of the population's money holdings and savings—appears unnecessary. Such a measure can be avoided if the current inflationary trend is reversed and confidence in the currency is gradually established.

A one-time elimination of excess demand cannot deal by itself with the problem of repressed inflation, nor can the exclusive reliance on monetary tightening or a zero-deficit fiscal policy. Institutional changes must be included not only to restore momentary equilibrium, but also to maintain long-term balance and confidence.

Another problem is the continuing dearth of appropriate instruments for private savers. The real interest on savings deposits is negative, the bond market is highly unstable, no attention was paid to small savers in the various privatization schemes, and the small company sector suffers from extensive bureaucratic obstacles. For practical and legal reasons (including a lack of information and transparency), most savers have no access to the numerous forms of more or less speculative investment schemes. The anti-inflationary program should be closely coordinated with the objectives of creating private capital and gradual privatization. *A careful, innovative, and intelligent approach to privatization could greatly help to tie down excess liquidity held by the public. This would certainly be a more auspicious beginning for the market economy than destroying (through inflation or confiscation) personal savings.*

Obviously, such a policy has to be both socially equitable and economically reasonable. In the long run, the elimination of future sources of leakages and of distortions will help create and maintain confidence. These institutional changes need not and cannot be carried out in a single operation. The long-term objective has to be clearly defined, and institutional changes and day-to-day policy have to be compatible and consistent with these long-term goals. A lasting solution has to be conducive to an effective increase in output and an improvement in the quality and range of goods and services available in Hungary. (Import liberalization and travel allowances represented a partial attempt of easing the pent-up demand or monetary overhang through an increase in the supply of imported goods, without increasing the output of the economy.)

ECONOMIC LIBERALIZATION, PROMOTING COMPETITION, AND AN EFFECTIVE WAGE AND PRICE POLICY

Increased competition and labor mobility and the liberalization of prices and wages in truly competitive sectors are essential to offsetting the impact of 40 years of distortions under the Socialist economic system and to providing the right incentives for private initiative and increased efficiency throughout the economy. Further progress in eliminating price and wage distortions is also important for the success of an anti-inflationary policy.

So far Hungary has made progress in liberalizing consumer and industrial prices as well as wages. New legislation has been prepared for the creation of an office of Competition and Monopoly Control, the elimination of most price restrictions, and a new approach to price surveillance related to unfair competition.

The effectiveness of adopted or proposed measures depends on the objectives being pursued and on the conditions in various sectors and in the economy as a whole. However, in light of the record of price increases in the last two years and of the experience of early 1990, it is important to point out once more, given the structure of the economy, the absolute necessity for a continued active price and wage policy in Hungary.

As also argued by Hungarian specialists, price or wage liberalization must not help inefficient producers escape from market pressures, nor allow monopolists to maintain their economic power and to achieve substantial windfall profits. A simple bargaining mechanism will not be sufficient to prevent the recurrence of the dangers mentioned above. Thus, the control of prices and wages in companies where there is no effective competition should be enforced.

It is at least as important to prevent the development of a labor monopoly by the unions as it is to reduce or eliminate monopoly power among companies. A degree of cooperation on the part of organized labor will be necessary for checking cost inflation and for stimulating labor mobility. *However, without official influence over the supply and prices of basic goods and services, a labor peace (for example, of the kind that existed in Germany after the war or that has prevailed in Switzerland for over 50 years) will be very difficult to achieve.*

REFORM OF THE FINANCIAL, MONETARY, AND BANKING SYSTEM

A credible monetary, banking, and financial system is the basis of a modern, growing economy. Creating the basis and the instruments of an effective monetary policy has to be high on the agenda of economic reform and economic policy. This is the precondition for checking inflation and for maintaining a stable national currency. It is also indispensable for the development of a realistic price structure and of financial markets favorable to domestic savings.

■ The Hungarian Financial System

As in all Socialist and planned economies, the banking and financial system in Hungary had been basically flawed for decades. The ultimate decisions concerning financial resources were centralized in the State budget. The central organs of the State withdrew surpluses from individual companies and sectors (and from households), and they attributed resources to individual firms, sectors, administrations, or in favor of households and of consumption, out of the State budget. The criteria for determining the surplus and attributions were adopted on the basis of the plan's targets and preferences, rather than market performance and prices.

As a result of a series of reforms—including the decentralization of production decisions to the company level, the creation of a two-tiered banking system, and the introduction of a tax system—this model no longer corresponds fully to the Hungarian reality. Sufficiently important elements seem to exist, however, to make further reform indispensable.

Despite the creation of a two-tiered banking system and of certain new policy instruments, the impact of monetary policy remains uneven. The Hungarian National Bank has a dual role, and its tasks as the accounting branch of the state budget still seem to predominate. Although in principle it has at its disposal various new monetary policy instruments, so far it has not been able to pursue a consistent monetary policy because of various leakages in the system. Its main responsibilities include the task of borrowing abroad the resources required by the economy, i.e., essentially by the state budget. A significant portion of available financial resources has been attributed to the State Development Institute, which is responsible for financing large projects.

Thus, transparency and accountability in the collection and the distribution of resources are still lacking. This process is still influenced by arbitrary, political, or personal (bargaining) decisions. Although interest rates have begun to affect both savers and borrowers, it is difficult to assess their effective role in economic decisions. The current rate of inflation exacerbates this situation and makes it more difficult to apply objective, economically rational criteria.

Until very recently, there have been no clear positive incentives for financial performance and for the efficient management of resources, neither at the level of state-owned or subsidized enterprises nor in public services and investments (nor have there been effective sanctions for wasteful management). The instruments and incentives for savings are not very effective in the current economic and financial climate. In the recent past, foreign currencies and real estate have proved to be the most reliable instruments of savings.

The balance sheets of both banks and companies are basically flawed since the valuation of assets and liabilities is also based on arbitrary criteria. This results not only from the lack of new, uniform accounting rules, but also from the uncertainty of ownership control and the principles and practice of so-called "spontaneous" privatization.

Although most people are badly hurt by inflation, the system also creates considerable windfall profits, in particular through real estate and currency speculation. Because of the loss of confidence in the currency, the extent of the monetary overhang in the economy cannot be measured through the traditional statistics of the money supply. There is a widespread impression in the country that inflation and the difficulty of distinguishing between good and bad assets (and between good and bad loans) tend to favor the efforts of the rulers to consolidate their economic situation at the expense of the average wage earner.

■ Main Objectives of the Reform

The first and most important objective is to provide an efficient and equitable system for the collection and distribution of the scarce financial resources in the economy. The basic principle has to be that of the market economy. This implies (a) an adequate (market-conforming) retribution or price (interest payments, dividends, appreciation of assets, etc.) for the owners of the financial resources (savers); (b) equally market-conforming payments by the users of the resources (investors, companies, other borrowers, and users including the state and its various subsidiaries); (c) a neutral and objective system (i.e., market) for the distribution of the financial resources (i.e., outside the state budget, and outside a personal or corporate bargaining system); and (d) freedom of access to the market for both savers and borrowers.

A second objective, closely linked to the first, is domestic and external monetary stability. Monetary stability is essential for the currency to fulfil its three main functions: a means of exchange, a measure of value, and a store of value. Broad monetary stability (which does not mean administratively fixed, rigid prices) is necessary to avoid price distortions in the economy and the occurrence of unearned profits and economically unjustified losses.

Finally, the system has to be trustworthy, transparent, and reliable. There should be no room for private or public abuses of economic and financial power and for the careless or corrupt handling of other people's money. So-called "insider deals" (concerning credits or the purchase or sale of financial or other assets) can discredit the market and the banks as much in a small and newly created financial system as in the largest and most highly developed economy. Monetary policy, the banking sector, and the financial markets should not be subject to directives from the government, Parliament, or political parties in their business decisions. The financial markets have to be altogether outside the budget. However, the public sector is responsible for the adoption and enforcement of strict rules of behavior, and in particular, for the protection of small savers against both expropriation and illegal or unethical business practices.

■ Main Tasks of the Reform

Since the components of the monetary, banking, and financial system are interconnected, the institutional reform and the financial consolidation have to take into account both the functional specificity and the macroeconomic homogeneity of banking and finance.

Changing the Financial Role of the Goverment.   In all economies, the government and the central bank have the primary responsibility for monetary stability, but their relative responsibility varies, as does the relative autonomy of the central bank. In the change from a Socialist to a market economy, a greater degree of success is likely if the central bank is given the degree of autonomy and responsibility under the Constitution as, for example, that enjoyed in the Federal Republic of Germany by the Bundesbank.

One of the central features of the metamorphosis of a Socialist economy into a market economy is the fundamental transformation of the financial functions of the government and the operation and criteria for budget decisions and their control. In Hungary some of this transformation, which cannot be completed in a few months without creating excessive social and economic costs, has begun already.

An immediate task in the post-election period will be to define clearly the goals, methods, and timeframe of this transformation and the operating rules (checks and balances) of the new system. This task will also include a thorough revision of the current procedures for infrastructure planning and financing.

Even in a time of great financial stringency and a severe austerity program that hits hard vast segments of Hungarian society, the former government appears willing to consider, without a thorough cost/benefit analysis, major prestige investment projects. Such projects would consume important domestic resources and swell Hungary's external debt, without a corresponding increase in the country's productive and financing capacity. In this process, the Hungarian authorities, as in the 1970s, seemed to be receiving considerable support and encouragement from abroad.

Transparency and accountability concerning public finance are of prime importance (*la vérité des comptes*). Parliament and elected regional and local bodies ought to have the responsibility for overall decisions and for the control of their execution. This does not mean, however, that Parliament (or the parties represented in Parliament) should be involved in all detailed decisions concerning the budget or extra-budgetary functions. Some of these responsibilities have to be delegated to the government, others to autonomous agencies. The rule of transparency and accountability, however, has to be respected. For major decisions concerning changes in the system or large infrastructure and other investment projects, a special procedure of consultation and hearings should be adopted.

The accounts and the budget of the state-owned enterprises, including those providing basic services, have to be clearly separated from the general government budget.

In view of the already heavy external debt and interest burden incurred by Hungary, the scope for budget deficits and for long- and short-term government borrowing should be strictly circumscribed. Certainly subsidies in some sectors will remain indispensable, but they should be publicly justified and financed out of ordinary receipts. As suggested in the other sections of this chapter, the management of the forint counterpart of capital imports and of the external resource transfer must not be the exclusive responsibility of the Hungarian Parliament and the government.

Important institutional changes will be required in the organization of the government and the definition of the responsibilities of the ministries and government agencies for the efficient planning and implementation of policies. These changes, to be carried out from the start, should include the creation of a strong Ministry of Economics, the clear definition of the responsibilities of the Ministry of Finance, the creation of a Ministry of Industry and Technology, the creation of a separate Ministry of State-Owned Companies, the clear definition of the tasks of the Agency for Competition and Monopoly Control, and the preparation of a new plan for infrastructure development.

Creating a Strong and Autonomous Central Bank.   One of the basic requirements of economic reform in Hungary is the transformation of the Hungarian National Bank into a strong, modern, and autonomous central bank. The reform of the National Bank ought to be coordinated with the creation of the proposed long-term credit and development bank and the consolidation of the commercial banking system.

The full and effective autonomy of the National Bank with respect to both the government and Parliament has to be established and guaranteed in the Constitution. The management of the National Bank, appointed for long, non-revokable terms, should be in permanent and close contact with the government and with the relevant Parliamentary Commissions. However, it should not receive binding instructions, either from the government or from Parliament, with respect to the conduct of monetary policy.

The necessity of the autonomy of the central bank from direct political influence is shown in the current developments in Europe. It is generally recognized that a European central bank, to be able to fulfil its responsibilities, will have to be autonomous with respect to both the member governments and the European Commission.

The main tasks of the National Bank should be the safeguarding of the domestic and external stability of the forint, the effective macroeconomic control over the growth of credit in the economy, and participation in the supervision of a sound banking and financial industry. This means that the National Bank should withdraw from all long-term financing operations. At least part of the old long-term State debt should be consolidated and separated from the regular balance sheet of the National Bank; it might be transferred to a special account of the new Hungarian-International Long-Term Credit and Development Bank. Some of the counterpart funds from the debt adjustment could be used to consolidate the balance sheet of the National Bank; this would avoid a conflict of interest between the National Bank's responsibility for monetary stability and the potential political pressure for external financing of government spending. Following the consolidation phase and the eventual privatization of the Hungarian-International Long-Term Credit and Development Bank, the role of the central bank in this field could be reconsidered.

The National Bank ought to have a full range of instruments to carry out its tasks. In principle, the government's borrowing requirements ought to be financed through the markets. Thus, the conditions for short-term lending to the government and to the banks ought to be redefined.

Information about the objectives and policies pursued by the National Bank should be clearly and systematically presented. Experience has shown that a reliance on purely quantitative monetary objectives is not advisable because of the instability of the demand for money (velocity). Thus, in the design and implementation of its policies, the central bank should take into account both quantitative monetary targets and the evolution of interest rates, as is the case with the major continental central banks such as the Bundesbank. At the same time, it will have to resist pressures for "cheap money" policies and artificially low interest rates.

Consolidating the Banking System.   The 1987 reform created a series of commercial banks, the main task of which ought to be the provision of credit to the economy. At present, however, the ability of the banks to fulfil their tasks of financing the borrowing requirements of the economy, and as the collectors and managers of the surplus financial resources of the economy (enterprise sector and households), remains limited.

The banks, which still essentially belong to the state, are constrained by their weak capital base and by the large amount of bad or uncollectible debts carried on their balance sheets. Although on paper the banks have been highly profitable compared with industrial companies, they are as much in need of consolidation and reorganization as the rest of the economy and the public administration.

The principal consolidation tasks include

- Consolidating and reorganizing the banks' balance sheets, writing off bad debts, and injecting new capital. As in the case of the National Bank, this could be done partly with the help of counterpart funds from the debt relief operation.

- Defining clear rules of accounting and operations: rules of behavior concerning the use of bank and depositors' funds; rules concerning credit policies, including capital and lending ratios; rules governing the interbank market, minimum reserve requirements, and borrowing from the National Bank; the protection of savers and other depositors; the prohibition of insider deals; and the definition of prudent banking practices.

- Reorganizing bank surveillance.

Surveillance of the Banks and of Financial Markets.   It is arguable whether the task of banking supervision should be the responsibility of the central bank as in France and the United Kingdom, or of an independent organization. In either case, an active role for government is undesirable except as the proposer of legislation and perhaps in an appellate capacity. A separate, autonomous body may be in charge of supervising the stock exchange.

The rules with respect to various types of operations have to be defined with clarity and in the simplest terms possible. The right of issuing various types of savings instruments (various types of shares, convertible bonds, bonds, etc.) has to be clearly defined and its exercise subject to specific rules.

The development of a capital market has to be paralleled by the introduction of new common accounting practices. The particular conditions in Hungary present considerable temptation for insider deals. Whether they involve the management or allegedly outside consultants or investors (who are often former Ministry officials), such deals undermine the respect for private property and can be economically inefficient. This is one more reason why privatization has to be conceived as a gradual process.

In a thin, unexperienced, and excessively speculative market, the stock exchange could do more harm than good. Yet a well managed stock exchange and capital market are essential for the success of the transformation. The good reputation of the banks and of the Hungarian financial markets will be a precondition for the good reputation of the market economy in Hungary and abroad.

The long-term concept for Hungarian banks ought to mirror that of universal banks. Within such a system, there is room for the separate National Savings Bank, as well as for the specialized long-term credit and development bank proposed in this study.

The development of so-called institutional investors (insurance companies, pension funds, municipalities, and so forth) can be developed only slowly. At present they lack both the manpower and the experience for effectively carrying out financial market operations.

The Companies.   According to official Hungarian analyses, little has improved in the efficiency of Hungarian companies* in industry or agriculture, notwithstanding the earlier reform measures or the current financial pressures. This situation results from important leakages in the Hungarian financial and banking system on one hand, and on the other hand, from the absence of credible and enforceable sectorial policies of the kind that exist even in many of the most liberal OECD economies.

One of the principal leakages of the Hungarian financial system has been the expansion of intercompany lending and especially of loans forced by illiquidity or inability to pay. The system of so-called "queuing" (where the unpaid bills are arranged according to their due dates) is the result both of poor performance and of the strict credit restrictions applied to the productive sector. According to some estimates, the volume of forced loans amounts currently to 400 billion forints, roughly the equivalent of the commercial banks' lending to the economy at the end of 1988.

---

*The term "companies" is meant to include the cooperatives.

The practice of inter company lending is dangerous both from a macroeconomic and from a microeconomic point of view. It weakens the impact of monetary policy. It allows operation with regard to capital adequacy, valuations rules, taxes, and so forth, and it hampers the discipline of pricing and the transparency needed for honest management and ownership control. Thus, intercompany transactions should be prohibited for any credits beyond 90 days (trade credits), on a nonrenewable basis. In *rare* cases, exceptions could be granted by the central bank. The use, for example, of short-term promissory notes, the use and quality of which would have to be controlled by the commercial banks and which could be rediscounted with the central bank, would provide an appropriate means of commercial financing and of control of the financial practices of enterprises.

The process of unwinding the queuing system may involve the bankruptcy of a number of companies. To avoid waste and unnecessary asset destruction, the adoption of an orderly bankruptcy procedure is in the interests of the Hungarian economy. Such a procedure will require both macroeconomic and microeconomic measures. It will have to be coordinated with the reorganization and the consolidation of the banking system.

The reorganization of the productive sector in Hungary cannot be accomplished only through bankruptcies and financial disincentives. Many companies are no doubt beyond hope. However, in many cases the inefficiencies have been condoned or perhaps inadvertently encouraged by wrong signals or incentives coming from the business environment. The decision to close down or reorganize (new management, staff cutbacks, capital injection, and so forth) will have to take into account the current market situation, as well as the longer term perspectives of the Hungarian economy. The interest of potential foreign partners or buyers (or of Hungarian investors) is an important factor, but should not be the sole determinant of the decision. Nor can the decision be left completely either to foreign consultants or accountants or to a bargaining process between managers and government officials.

In fact, without returning to a planned economy, the reform of the Hungarian economy will also have to include sectorial concepts—at least the concept of an industrial policy and an agricultural policy—which will provide general guidelines (but not unlimited financial support) when dealing with specific companies.

PROMOTION OF SAVINGS AND PRIVATE PROPERTY, PRIVATIZATION AND FOREIGN DIRECT INVESTMENTS
■ Promoting and Protecting Savings

An anti-inflationary policy is also an essential requirement of an active promotion of savings. At approximately one quarter of the Gross Domestic Product (GDP), Hungary's savings rate is not low. Although in a growing economy it might be possible to raise the savings rate further, the key issue is not the level of savings, but as argued throughout the present report, the wasteful use of resources, including savings. Internal and external balance cannot be established merely by putting pressure on consumption. Private incomes are very low, and the resulting low consumption cannot be further reduced without seriously hurting the country's social fabric and thereby reducing the motivation to innovate and to work harder. Hungary is not over-consuming in any real sense of the word but badly investing and therefore under- or misproducing.

Increased private ownership, based on effective profits and savings, is a central issue in the development of a stable market economy. Improving the incentives for savings is both a short-term and long-term objective. It is necessary to reduce or tie down the current monetary overhang in the economy, and in the long-run to provide the capital necessary for the growth of the Hungarian economy.

The promotion of household savings (which represent about 14 percent of the GDP) and the accumulation of private capital are both an economic and a political necessity in Hungary. They will restore the people's economic autonomy, and thus their social and political responsibility, thereby providing the necessary resources for creating and restoring the country's productive and infrastructure capital. A positive initiative was made in this direction in the field of housing, where home ownership in the cities and in the rural areas has helped offset to some extent the dismal situation of council housing. In the field of housing as in other forms of capital accumulation, it is important to avoid favoritism or social inequities.

The most effective ways for promoting savings are the gradual reduction of public sector deficits and increased corporate profits. It is necessary to develop and strengthen the capital market (where the state will also have to finance its borrowing requirements). As far as private savings are concerned, it will be necessary to provide positive interest on savings deposits and to innovate and develop new instruments available for households (e.g., convertible securities linked to the privatization of companies, participation certificates, home-ownership, year-end productivity related bonus system, and so forth). Tax incentives for savings have to be provided for both companies and households.

Personal savings require more innovation than high real interest rates, with equity appreciation potentially the most promising in Hungary. A key instrument could be convertible bonds, which would ensure some income and substantial future capital gains, or bonds with attached warrantees.

It will be essential to innovate with regard to capital formation, and eventually even to subsidize some forms of equity savings. This should be linked to the elimination of excess liquidity and to the broadening of the financing capacity of private enterprises. This could involve tax benefits for bonus systems with equity participation, issuing small denomination shares, investment funds, and so forth. *In the process of privatization, the Hungarian public should have an opportunity to buy at least part of the shares. This general principle ought to be included into the law and not left to the discretion of bureaucrats or of a parliamentary commission.*

The promotion of savings could be a key topic for Task Force Hungary and a Working Party, in view of the broad and successful experience of countries like Germany, France, Japan, or the United Kingdom.

■ Checking Excessive Speculation

Creating a healthy capital market is one of the priorities in Hungary. Without a rational collection and distribution of the (scarce) available resources, there is no chance for the growth and modernization of the Hungarian economy. The task is not to create sophisticated financial institutions and instruments, copied from recent innovation in large and highly developed financial markets, but to assure that the basic institutions and rules of the financial system are well defined and function correctly.

It is necessary to develop the instruments and markets of savings and of ownership titles, as well as to make these instruments as easily transferable as possible. It is more important to develop and to protect the substance than to copy foreign models of financial instruments and create illusions of financial sophistication. If the reform of the Hungarian economy succeeds, there is likely to be a very important appreciation of productive assets and of ownership titles to these assets. Yet, in an economy like that of Hungary at present, an excessive emphasis on financial or real estate speculation (by foreign or domestic actors), at the expense of productive investment, risk financing, or venture capital financing, must be avoided.

Today, the main stimulants of purely speculative activity (as distinguished from the necessary restructuring and modernization of the economy) are inflation, the lack of clear and transparent accounting practices and valuation criteria, and confused ownership conditions. It is urgent to deal with all three to prevent the spreading of an unhealthy speculative climate, which would hurt Hungarian entrepreneurs, arrest the development of the capital market, and discourage productive foreign direct investments.

In fact, widespread financial speculation would divert resources from the financing of trade and investments and complicate the task from the point of view of both the potential borrowers and of the lending institutions. In a country with great resource scarcity and considerable financing needs by both new and existing companies, this could be a major deterrent to growth, especially in the creation and expansion of new, possibly highly leveraged companies.

There is also an important psychological reason for clarifying the distinction between the normal functioning of financial markets (with normal fluctuations in prices, values, and interest rates, the risks involved, and the role of the intermediaries) and excessive speculative activity. In a country where most people have only a very limited degree of familiarity with the rules and functioning of the market economy, excessive financial speculation could rapidly discredit the market economy and contribute to a political backlash.

A third reason is that few people could speculate with their own money. Speculating with other people's funds (or with one's company's funds) not only may be objectionable from a moral and legal point of view, but even more importantly, would be dangerous from a prudent economic point of view.

Finally, experience has shown that in countries with narrow markets and underdeveloped financial instruments, the spreading of financial speculation tends very rapidly to spill beyond the country's borders and turn into legal or illegal capital exports. Yet, conditions in the Hungarian economy and in the Hungarian financial system ought to be such that there would be no economic stimulation for capital exports in the foreseeable future. This can be achieved through monetary stability and proper financial rules and institutions, rather than through the promotion of financial speculation.

■ The Need for a Coherent Policy Toward Private and Public Enterprise

The outcome of three closely connected structural challenges will have a decisive impact on the country's economic performance:

- The creation and the promotion of genuine, new private enterprises

- The more rational and efficient management of state-owned companies

- The privatization of state-owned companies.

All three are long-term tasks for which it will be necessary to adopt clear policies and guidelines at the earliest possible date.

The creation and promotion of new Hungarian enterprises has to be of central concern to future economic policy. It will require special attention through the proposed new long-term bank, other financial and fiscal measures, the creation of appropriate infrastructures, the reduction of red tape, and so forth. Although many steps have been taken to encourage direct foreign investments in Hungary, it is widely argued that the measures to encourage the creation and growth of new Hungarian enterprises have been insufficient so far.

There is also a widespread (and probably well-founded) impression in Hungary and abroad that many of the rules and legislation adopted in recent months (including those related to the transformation into joint stock or limited responsibility companies and to the privatization and management of state-owned enterprises) have been rather hastily prepared or have been weakened under the pressure of various groups, including worker-managed companies.

The law about the new State Property Agency was conceived as a contribution to the essential and urgent task to halt the inefficient management of state-owned companies. According to the original text, the main task of this Agency should be the sale of state-owned assets according to annual programs to be defined by Parliament.

Privatization should contribute to the objective of increased efficiency, but it cannot be the only or initially even the principal instrument of achieving it. The new legislation to become effective on March 1, 1990, provides for increased government control of privatization (an authorization procedure, the right of veto, and the possibility of renationalization of worker-managed enterprises). However, increasing the efficiency in state-owned companies cannot wait for privatization. In fact, restructuring and consolidation often have to precede successful attempts at privatization.

The management concept defined in the legislation adopted in early 1990 is inspired by the idea of contracting out. This could take the form of companies, lease or rental, or of holding or management groups. Certain reservations are called for both with respect to the general concept and to its large-scale practical application. A decentralized management structure is necessary to respond to market incentives and pressures. As long as it is the owner, the state must not abdicate the ultimate responsibility for ensuring that the companies are run efficiently. The lessons from all European countries with state-owned companies prove that the public sector must not be a less demanding and less exacting owner than private investors. Public-sector companies must be subject to the same accounting and reporting rules as companies in the private sector. If they have financing needs, they also will have to turn to the market.

The idea to entrust the supervision of state-owned companies to independent or private management groups seems a questionable compromise between the trend throughout 1989 and the reassertion of the state's responsibility. It reflects the same kind of intellectual compromise as the "Socialist market economy" or the creation of worker-controlled companies.

In the first place, it would be an abdication and/or dilution of the government's responsibility. Instead of having to control the companies, government officials would have to control the management and the private supervisors as well. This solution offers all the temptations of a perfect insider deal. The idea that the private controllers would be responsible for securing a minimum annual profit for the state as an owner is unrealistic in a market economy. The guidelines defined by the owners have to be both more precise and more flexible. The boards of directors of state-owned companies may include private or independent experts. The state will have to appoint efficient managers, who could be removed if they were not achieving expected results. In turn, they should be paid salaries in line with the complexity of their assignments, in the form of bonuses and/or stock certificates.

There is also a need for more precise guidelines for privatization (which go beyond the organization of auctions) and supervision of the financial, legal, and industrial aspects. From a political point of view it is important to assure the public that no disbanding and giving-away of public property is taking place. Stripping assets and dispersing ownership and effective control without appropriate compensation to the collective, would be no way to start a market economy and to ensure the respect for private property.

This stricture applies also to the idea of handing out ownership titles in industrial or service companies to collective bodies (the social security fund, regional or municipal councils, hospitals, and so forth), i.e., to organizations as notoriously inefficient in their own fields as the production companies and that do not have any relevant experience whatsoever in effectively overseeing or running these companies.

Conversely, as mentioned above, effective measures ought to be devised for creating opportunities for popular share-holding as well as for direct interest (via stock bonuses, for example) of managers. *One of the most questionable features of the legislation on privatization and the State Property Agency is the absence of any explicit rules or reference to selling shares to small Hungarian investors and savers not affiliated with the companies concerned.* This reflects a basic (and often unjustified) lack of confidence both in the value of assets to be privatized and in the ability of Hungarian savers to make rational choices.

Privatization can only be a long-term process. It has to follow transparent and strict rules. It should be in the public interest through the sale price achieved and through increased output and productivity. A careless approach to privatization would discredit the market economy and lead to a corporatist and inefficient economic structure, with a negative impact on the growth potential of the economy.

The goals and priorities of privatization should be clearly stated. These should be increased competition, more efficient management, modernization, and increased private share-holding in Hungary.

Experience in Western Europe has shown that privatization makes more sense and is easier to implement in areas in which, under a market system, there is substantial competition, rather than in sectors in which, even in market economies, monopolies or near-monopolies predominate. In monopolies, privatization has to be accompanied by various regulatory devices that are often cumbersome and difficult. This experience has to be kept clearly in mind since, for reasons of political and economic convenience, there seems to be a temptation in Hungary to privatize large organizations and monopolies or near-monopolies first.

It is also difficult to understand, from a political and from an economic point of view, the *de facto* or legal barriers to the privatization of what are essentially small and medium-sized businesses such as retail commerce, restaurants, and small industrial activities that appear to belong to strong (often local or regional) monopolies.

The macroeconomic dimension of privatization must also be handled carefully. Receipts from privatization should not be spent for current consumption (neither by the state nor by the company being privatized); rather, a significant portion should be frozen to diminish excess liquidity. The amounts reinvested in the company should be subject to more precise rules and controls than currently exist.

■ Foreign Direct Investments

Hungary has rightly adopted a very liberal approach to joint ventures and foreign direct investments. This has created considerable interest among foreign investors, and numerous investment and joint-venture projects have been announced and implemented. Foreign direct investment can contribute in multiple ways to the modernization and development of the Hungarian economy, as it is contributing to the expansion of numerous industrialized and developing countries:

- Transferring financial resources

- Introducing experienced management and management methods

- Introducing and diffusing new technologies

- Integrating into European and world markets

- Achieving economies of scale at the level of production and of research and development.

A liberal and open attitude is essential, as is the provision of the necessary support and infrastructure. Although no "central plan" is possible or necessary for foreign investment, a well-defined policy is required to make the best of foreign investments. Today, Hungarian officials admit they are at a loss about what instruments to include in a direct investment policy; they are rightly anxious to avoid a planning approach. *Yet, they also need instruments to allow them to check the inflow of excessively speculative funds and the sale of intentionally or inadvertently underpriced assets. The justified or unjustified fear of wasting assets (Ausverkauf der Heimat) could stimulate economic nationalism in Hungary.* There is also a danger that speculative capital inflows will be used as a subterfuge for capital exports and capital flight. It is surprising to see that not only Hungarian liberals but also some of the Western advisers, seem to be oblivious to these potential threats.

Ultimately, Hungary should be primarily interested in investors seeking long-term commitments. A careful assessment of market value is essential. It is, however, also important to consider the industrial implications of investments. In the case of joint ventures or takeovers of existing Hungarian firms, potential investors that, beside financial resources, also have successful technologies and products and that can help integrate the Hungarian operations into their international production and sales network should receive encouragement. Foreign capital and enterprise skills should support domestic enterprise. Selling assets to foreign companies makes sense if the capital received is ploughed back into better wealth-creating activities and if the enterprises sold bring greater benefits to the country. Selling assets abroad is probably of little value if the main beneficiary in the years to come will be the foreign purchaser.

It follows that foreign purchases of Hungarian enterprises should be allowed and justified mainly in terms of the contribution these transactions will make in creating wealth for reinvestment domestically, in increasing exports and improving Hungary's international competitive position, as well as in terms of their ability to stimulate the general enterprise culture and level of technological development.

The need for the continuation of a careful, possibly restrictive, policy for foreign investments in Hungarian real estate should also be emphasized. Authorizations for purchases connected with productive investments or certain construction projects should be granted liberally, but the buying of factories ought not to be a pretext for real-estate speculation. At a time when the Hungarian currency is and will remain undervalued in terms of purchasing power comparisons, and when there is no transparent and properly functioning market for land and housing, a massive influx of foreign investment in Hungarian real estate could result in very unsettling social and economic consequences.

EXCHANGE RATE POLICY AND THE SCOPE OF CONVERTIBILITY

An appropriate exchange rate level is essential, both before and after the establishment of full convertibility. It should be determined on the basis of the general competitive position of the Hungarian economy and of a broad purchasing power comparison; it would be wrong to encourage inefficient exporters through a systematic undervaluation of the forint. As for imports, customs duties are a more flexible and more rational instrument of (temporary) protection than devaluation. It is also a dangerous illusion that a sufficiently drastic devaluation can create by itself the conditions for the successful establishment of full convertibility. More often than not, such a measure is likely to diminish rather than increase confidence in the national currency.

Hungary should not adopt a system of free-floating exchange rates, neither now nor in the future. Such a system would create the illusion of policy autonomy for Hungarian decision makers, increase inflationary pressures, and make more difficult the integration with the European and world economy. A broad orientation toward the European Currency Unit (ECU) would provide the necessary combination of flexibility and stability for the external value of the forint.

Currency convertibility for the liberalized segment of imports exists already. Hungarian authorities are right in pressing for the elimination of the price distortions in CMEA trade. It may be also argued that overall external trade convertibility would benefit Hungary and without draining its foreign exchange reserves.

The black market and a certain flight into foreign currencies are a sign of a lack of domestic confidence and of the lack of attractive, alternative instruments of savings. It is necessary to halt and reverse this trend if a financial breakdown is to be avoided. The solution, however, is not the "big bang" approach of the Polish, Yugoslav, or Argentine models.

Full current account convertibility cannot happen at the start of the stabilization process, nor should it be postponed indefinitely. Convertibility for current transactions, including households, should be an important policy goal for the Hungarian government and its external partners. However, this goal cannot be achieved without domestic confidence and stability, balanced external accounts, and sufficient external reserves. Without domestic confidence in the national currency, convertibility is an invitation to capital flight for rich and poor savers alike.

What is needed now is a more rational access to foreign currencies for both companies and households. The new system of travel allocations is both humiliating and too complex and inefficient. It encourages the further development of the black market in foreign exchange. The real rate of return has to increase in Hungary not only for foreigners, but also for Hungarian savers and investors. However, establishing convertibility for capital transactions is a very long-term process requiring not only monetary stability, but also a high degree of integration in the international economy. It has taken several decades, since the late 1950s, for most of the Western European countries to achieve it.

Thus, capital movements will have to be monitored. Foreign investors should enjoy full convertibility, but any loopholes for capital flight should be closed. Reporting requirements (and approval under certain conditions) for direct investments should be maintained. Convertibility for capital transactions for Hungarian companies or private households cannot be attempted in the near future. However, even if controls are maintained, a certain liberalization may be justified for investments to promote the exports of Hungarian companies and their integration into the international economy.

THE TRANSFORMATION OF THE HUNGARIAN ECONOMY

Hungary is in a phase of transition from the most liberal of the Socialist economies to one being assessed as a potential market economy. While making a determined break with the past, it is also saddled with the inheritance of more than 40 years of distortions brought about by a command economy and by courageous but piecemeal and often erratic reform attempts. Now Hungary is simultaneously faced with a shortage of resources, and macroeconomic and microeconomic disequilibria.

The correction of the microeconomic distortions (i.e., toward the right products produced at the right prices using the right inputs and the right kind of technology) is seen as the principal source of future economic growth. This is recognized as a central objective of economic reform and economic policies. At the same time, there is also an obvious need to tackle the external and internal macroeconomic imbalance—to check inflation, to reduce fiscal leakages and excessive transfer payments, as well as to correct the imbalances in the country's balance of payments.

There is a need for carefully balanced macroeconomic, microeconomic, and social policies. It would be, in fact, equally unrealistic to assume that either fiscal or monetary largesse or massive capital imports, on the one hand, or an excessive reliance on fiscal and monetary austerity, on the other hand, could provide the overall conditions required for progress toward microeconomic balance and sustained economic growth.

Open or concealed inflation, whether from shortages or the artificial injection of purchasing power, is a source of major macroeconomic and microeconomic distortions. Similarly, the thesis that a massive reduction of living standards and the pauperization of large segments of society are necessary for the market economy to take off is socially unacceptable in a poor country like Hungary. It is also poor economics.

The Loss of Momentum
of the Hungarian Economy

According to official statistics, at current exchange rates the Hungarian GDP in 1989 was of the order of HF1650, or about $27 to 28 billion. With a total population of about 10.6 million, the per capita GDP of Hungary is about $2550. Among the OECD countries, only Turkey's is lower. Portugal, the next lowest among the OECD countries, has a per capita GDP about 20 percent higher than Hungary. The share of industry in the GDP is about 35 percent, and that of agriculture and forestry about 20 percent. The estimates for the "gray" or "parallel" economy vary between 10 and 25 percent of GDP, or perhaps more.

The 1980s witnessed a substantial deceleration of the Hungarian economy. Compared with an average annual growth of 4.6 percent during the 1970s, the GDP in constant prices increased by less than 1.5 percent p.a. during the 1980s. The low growth in the 1980s was in especially sharp contrast to the 6.3 percent growth performance of the 1966–1975 period. In 1988 and 1989 there was a virtual stagnation of the GDP. In 1990 this stagnation is expected to continue.

The situation has been even more unfavorable from the point of view of the domestic use of resources. During the 1980s it grew on the average by only 0.6 percent p.a., compared with an average annual growth of 4.0 percent during the 1970s.

As a result, the total domestic use of resources at the end of the 1980s was about 30 percent lower than it would have been if the growth trend of the 1970s had continued during the last 10 years. This comparison provides a quantitative illustration of the current domestic resource problem, or bottleneck, from the point of view of both consumption and investments. Measured in current prices, the difference for the single year 1989, between the actual domestic use of GDP and the level it would have reached with a 4.0 percent average growth through the 1980s, represented about $8 billion, or the equivalent of 40 percent of the country's gross external debt.

Average monthly wages are equivalent to $130 at current official exchange rates. The minimum monthly wage is equivalent to about $70.

THE SOURCES OF THE CURRENT MARASMUS

Several domestic and external factors have contributed to the poor growth record of the 1980s. To outside observers it has been evident that the systemic problems inherent even in a liberal Socialist economy weighed more heavily than the simple policy errors of the kind that also occur in a market economy.

Among the external developments, the deterioration of Hungary's terms of trade and the sharp rise in the cost of servicing the external debt have contributed prominently to the economic slowdown. These problems were compounded by the switch from heavy resource transfers *toward* Hungary in the 1970s to substantial net resource transfers *from* Hungary in the 1980s. Obviously, this has not prevented the Hungarian external debt from doubling during 1980s, as was also the case for a number of other heavily indebted countries during the same period.

The weakness of demand in the 1980s of many Third World markets, toward which Hungary had been trying to orientate its exports (markets that were considered to be less demanding in terms of quality, technical features, and precision of delivery, and more interested in barter), was an unexpected development for Hungarian leaders and planners. The emergence of the information society, the globalization of markets, and the greater emphasis on flexibility and quality throughout the world economy added to the handicaps faced by all Socialist economic systems. The earlier strong emphasis on the arms industry in Hungary as in the other Communist countries, and the weakening of worldwide demand in this sector, should also be mentioned.

The lackluster growth performance of the 1980s and the stop-go macroeconomic policies that followed have not helped bring about domestic or external equilibrium. As in many other countries in the past, the marasmus in the real economy increased rather than decreased the imbalances.

The principal factors responsible for the poor growth performance were of a structural nature: maintaining the planned economy, the central decision system for the distribution of financial and other resources, and a distorted price system. For example, until the 1980s the impact of the rise in oil prices had been corrected through subsidies (and, in fact, through borrowing abroad).

It is rightly argued that in the 1970s insufficient use had been made of capital imports to modernize the Hungarian economy. There was, obviously, also a waste of foreign resources through consumption. This higher level of consumption (which never really became excessive in Western European terms), however, also had a positive impact. It contributed to a certain nonpolitical internal consensus that ultimately helped prepare the conditions for a radical but peaceful change in the country, once the external constraints appeared to be relaxed. The greater scope for private consumption also played a powerful role in the development of the parallel or gray economy, the first real manifestation of true private initiative in several decades. Finally, the waste through a limited availability of imported consumer goods and through more liberal travel possibilities than any other Eastern European country, was at least partly offset by the access it allowed for managers, scientists, and the average citizen to the outside world. That exposure ought to help Hungarians in their current attempt to develop a dynamic market economy.

The housing situation remains a major problem, in particular because of the neglected and run-down condition of council housing. Nevertheless, as a result of the increased availability and encouragement of private home ownership (and since private home-building has been a major field for the expansion of the private or semiprivate economy), there has been a significant improvement in the general situation, in particular outside Budapest.

The wasteful management of stocks and raw materials also remained pervasive, and the widespread waste on the side of productive and infrastructure investments are often noted. In the 1970s and 1980s, a series of important investment errors occurred in energy and in prestige projects in other sectors. The inability to realize the importance of telecommunications for the modern economy has been a good illustration of the arbitrary selection of major investment projects well into the 1980s and the predominance of ideological considerations at the top.

The survival of this type of thinking and the lure of mammoth prestige projects was vividly shown at the end of 1989. At the time when the government was seeking approval of its austerity plan, in view of the severe balance-of-payment situation and shortage of foreign reserves, it obtained parliamentary approval for the planned $3 billion Vienna-Budapest World Exhibition, invoking both the alleged economic benefits and the prestige and "the opening" to Europe that the project was hoped to bring for Hungary.

Until very recently one of the most wasteful systemic problems has been the virtual impossibility for entrepreneurs in the gray economy to invest and to own capital. This represented a major limitation on the expansion of this sector, and in most cases kept it at a low technological and management level (which has not always been the case for the gray economies of some of the Southern European countries). Although now legally possible, the access for genuine private entrepreneurs to capital remains difficult as a result of the tight money policy. The widespread practice of borrowing tools and equipment from state-owned companies to be used in the parallel economy during or outside working hours (which has been the reason for many people to stay on at their official jobs) has contributed to the general waste and to the corruption of work habits in the Socialist sector.

FOREIGN TRADE AND THE BALANCE OF PAYMENTS

A strategy of export-led growth seems a reasonable course of action for Hungary in the years to come. Such a development is desirable not only because of the country's external financial situation; through the business and technological integration with the world economy, it will also help upgrade the quality of the domestic market. Its chances of success depend on the development of private initiative and less wasteful management in the state-owned companies, effective control of inflation, the unification of prices in the domestic, dollar, and CMEA markets, the growth of foreign direct investments in Hungary, and trade policy measures in favor of Hungary by the OECD countries.

Even today, the achievements of the Hungarian economy, in foreign trade terms, are remarkable, given the general and systemic constraints under which it has had to operate. Thus, the degree of international integration of the Hungarian economy is relatively high. Currently, total exports of goods and services are close to 40 percent of GDP in current prices, and about 50 percent in constant, 1981 prices. Since 1980 there has been a deterioration of Hungary's terms of trade by about 10 percent, in contrast to the OECD countries, which saw during this period a significant improvement, or at least a stabilization, of their terms of trade.

In 1988, the Socialist countries accounted for 49 percent of the value of Hungarian merchandise imports and for 50.5 percent of Hungarian exports (in rubles and convertible currencies). The foreign trade in (nonconvertible) rubles amounted to 43 percent of imports and 41 percent of exports in 1988. From $95 million in 1988, the trade surplus in nonconvertible currencies rose to $507 million in 1989. This was the result mainly of supply difficulties encountered by the Soviet economy, but also of the unwillingness of Hungarian companies to reduce their exports in nonconvertible currencies.

The share of the developed market economies was close to 44 percent of Hungarian imports, and 40.5 percent of Hungarian exports. Hungarian trade with the European Community represented 25 percent of imports and 22 percent of total exports. Next to the Soviet Union, the Federal Republic of Germany is Hungary's principal trading partner.

As for the commodity structure of foreign trade, over 20 percent is food and agricultural products, compared with less than 5 percent on the import side. Hungary's most pronounced dependence on the CMEA trade is in energy imports—90 percent of total energy imports and 12 percent of total merchandise imports. On the export side, food and agricultural exports (partly in convertible currencies) to the USSR accounted for 7 percent of total Hungarian exports (over 30 percent of exports in this category) and 23 percent of total exports to the Soviet Union. A pronounced export dependence vis-à-vis the Soviet Union and other CMEA can be observed also for machinery and investment goods exports. Ruble exports in this category (probably including arms exports) amounted to over 72 percent of the total of this category and for 20 percent of total Hungarian exports.

Tourism has been an important source of income for several years, both from Western tourists and from visitors from other Socialist countries who used to represent a captive market for Hungary. In 1989 there was, however, a sharp deterioration in the tourism accounts, with a major shift from a traditional surplus to a large deficit, as a result of the liberalization of foreign travel regulations. A substantial share of the travel expenses, however, represented direct imports of consumer goods, especially of durable consumer goods, by Hungarian households.

According to preliminary data for 1989, the trade balance in convertible currencies showed a surplus of over $540 million (compared with $490 million in 1988), despite a certain import liberalization (mainly affecting machinery and equipment). The current account in convertible currencies, however, registered a $1.4 billion deficit as a result of the net interest payments and the deterioration of the travel balance. The current account surplus in nonconvertible currencies was estimated at 1.8 billion rubles, or about $820 million equivalent at the official forint-ruble exchange rate.

Thus, the total trade surplus, in convertible and nonconvertible currencies, was of the order of $1.1 billion, or about 4 percent of GDP. The surplus of the combined current account in convertible and nonconvertible currencies, taking into account the deterioration on the travel account, but before interest payments, was the equivalent of close to 2.5 percent of the GDP.

Since the ruble surplus cannot be used to finance the convertible current account deficit, there was a deterioration of $1.4 billion in Hungary's external financial position in convertible currencies. In other words, if Hungary had tried to avoid a convertible currency deficit in 1989 (by not granting the travel allowances) and an increase in its foreign indebtedness, it would have run a combined current account surplus before interest payments of the order of close to 6 percent of GDP, a large amount in a stagnating economy.

If there had been amortization of the external debts falling due (a theoretical proposition that must be considered in view of the cumulative burden of the heavy interest payments), an additional $2 billion would have had to be added to the current account surplus. The total resource transfer would have amounted to close to 10 percent of GDP.

The developments in 1989 have demonstrated more sharply than ever one of the central economic problems of the Socialist economies, the existence of three markets and of three sources of supply: (1) the domestic market; (2) the market of the CMEA countries, and supply from the Soviet Union and other Socialist countries; and (3) the Western, convertible-currency markets and sources of supply. Today, important differences continue to exist for these three markets from the point of view of the level and structure of prices; the availability, intensity, and regularity of supply; the quality requirements; and the external and domestic financing conditions.

Traditionally, the CMEA market has been the most rigid, and from a national point of view the least profitable. Because of the inherent rigid business practices, the uncertain delivery dates, the nonconvertible payments system, and the low quality and technological standards and requirements, this market contrasts sharply with the Western market and with the domestic Hungarian market.

In 1989 these problems have been aggravated by the increasing supply problems in the Soviet Union, which gives rise to considerable concern in

Hungary, particularly in view of the country's energy dependence on the USSR. In the trade for finished products, the rigid, officially fixed price structure has proven to be a major obstacle to quality improvements and product upgrading. At the same time, from the point of view of Hungarian exporters, the CMEA is the easiest market. In addition to the strong demand in the Soviet Union and the other member countries for Hungarian products, Hungarian ruble exports have been subsidized both directly and indirectly through favorable payments conditions.

Currently, the CMEA problem is seen both as a macroeconomic problem, in that the export surplus contributes to the excess demand and the inflationary pressures in the economy, and as a major microeconomic problem, in that it limits flexibility and slows the adaptation of Hungarian exporters to world market conditions and prices. It is also a political problem with respect to the Soviet Union and the other Eastern European countries.

As for the convertible currency markets, there is a certain amount of unsatisfied demand for both goods and foreign travel. This demand could not be dealt with through devaluation alone, as it is difficult to assess its price elasticity. This problem is compounded by the precautionary or speculative demand for foreign currency holdings as a result of the domestic inflationary expectations. Moreover, the inconvertible currency surplus also tends to add to the demand for convertible currencies because of the dollar content of the ruble exports and because of the income it generates.

In view of its large volume, it will be important to maintain trade with the CMEA countries, both on the supply side (energy, raw materials, and some finished products) and on the export side (food and manufactured products). At the same time, the continued existence of two types of foreign trade standards could jeopardize the success of the domestic reform.

The solution of the problem of CMEA trade has to be sought both domestically and internationally. Two simultaneous avenues seem appropriate: reduce the subsidies and favorable payment conditions for exports to CMEA countries and revalue the forint exchange rate; and seek convertibility for a growing share of the trade, not only with the more liberal CMEA countries like Poland, the emerging Czechoslovakia, and (the former) East Germany, but also with the Soviet Union.

As mentioned above, it is necessary to devise a careful strategy for progress towards full current account convertibility. The exchange rate does play an important role in helping bring the supply and demand for foreign currency into equilibrium; in no economy, however large or small, can it accomplish this task by itself. Although it is important that an overvaluation should be avoided, even a systematic undervaluation of the currency by itself will not bring the balance of payments into equilibrium. A policy of excessive devaluation, while fuelling domestic inflation, may encourage rather than slow the flight into foreign currency. The danger of capital flight must not be underestimated; both individual savers and institutions such as the commercial banks and the so-called autonomous companies will be susceptible. Any laxness on this account by the authorities could create lasting damage to the Hungarian economy.

Exchange rate policy ought to be aimed initially at assuring the price competitiveness of Hungarian exports, and at ensuring that imported products do not become excessively cheap through overvaluation. However, because of the tendency of purchasing power comparisons between more advanced and less advanced countries to go against the latter, the medium- to long-term objective of economic policy ought be a gradual revaluation of the exchange rate of the Hungarian currency.

THE SOURCES OF INFLATION

As mentioned above, since 1987 there has been a significant acceleration of inflation. Official projections for 1990 expect a 20 percent average increase in the cost of living; the effective rate could turn out to be significantly higher. Within this average, the price increases for basic goods and services (especially meat, rent, transportation, and telecommunications) will be much higher, on the order of 30 to 40 percent. The trend of industrial producer price increases has been significantly slower than that of consumer prices. As for export prices, prices of convertible currency exports increased more or less in line with inflation, whereas ruble export prices declined.

The inflation of recent years has been a new development, compared with a relatively satisfactory price performance during the 1970s and the first half of the 1980s. *Nevertheless the danger remains that a general inflationary mentality will spread. Some people privately or publicly favor a policy of letting things loose in the mistaken belief that a strong dose of inflation could miraculously create the basis for future confidence in the currency and an efficient production structure based on realistic market prices. Advocates of this "big bang" theory can be found not only among foreign academic economists, but also among some Hungarians.*

As usual, inflation in Hungary is attributable to several sources. At the structural level, the gradual liberalization of consumer prices and the reduction of price subsidies have to be mentioned. By the end of 1988 about 80 percent of consumer prices were freed and 20 percent were authority determined. The share of free prices has increased substantially, which has been reflected in the sharp increases in the prices of basic commodities and services announced in early 1990.

At the level of costs, wage increases, the actual or anticipated reduction of government subsidies, as well as the impact of forint devaluations should be pointed out. The wage adjustments on the occasion of the introduction of income taxes provided an initial wage push. The introduction of a value-added tax (VAT) initially amplified this development. The increase in the cost of living and the liberalization of wages have also led to a certain anticipatory wage inflation. In addition, in the absence of effective competition and budget control at the enterprise level, the cutbacks in subsidies tend to be passed on directly into higher prices. At the same time, even loss-making companies have been able to grant wage increases in line with the cost-of-living increases without reducing employment.

On the demand side, the principal sources of inflation are the government budget and the financial behavior of companies and cooperatives. As for the government budget, the principal problems have been financing the deficit through the National Bank, spending on huge projects (in particular in the energy sector), and subsidies to the productive sector and to households. The absence of spending discipline (wages, financial investments, machinery purchases, and inventory build-up) by unprofitable companies and cooperatives has been countenanced by the indiscriminate government subsidies to inefficient producers and by the lack of effective financial sanctions (market sanctions or ownership sanctions, or monetary sanctions against excessive intercompany lending).

MONETARY POLICY AND LEAKAGES IN THE SYSTEM

In 1988 and 1989 the Hungarian National Bank adopted the principle of a restrictive monetary policy. The main instruments of this policy have been the reduction of the refinancing quotas of the commercial banks with the National Bank and the increase of the interest rate charged to the banks for borrowing from the National Bank. As a result, the level of bank credits to the economy declined by more than 6 percent in 1988 (credits by the large commercial banks diminished by over 10 percent) in current prices. Taking into account inflation, the decline in constant prices amounted to 20 to 25 percent. In 1989 the volume of credit increased, but more slowly than the inflation rate.

The monetary tightness hit hardest (directly and indirectly) the official and inofficial firms working for the domestic consumer and convertible currency markets. At the same time, however, there have been important leakages in the system. The first factor is the increase in the government's budget deficit in 1988 and 1989, financed essentially by the National Bank. The enterprises fulfilling their planned exports to the ruble market also largely escaped from the consequences of the tight monetary policies partly through the mechanism of direct subsidies and partly because they were automatically given the forint counterpart of the value of their nonconvertible exports. It should also be noted that a substantial portion of the productive sector has been immune to the tightening of bank credits, since it receives its financial resources directly from the government budget. Thus, up until last year, 40 percent of Hungarian companies did not have recourse to bank financing. The sharp increase in the surplus of the nonconvertible current account surplus, financed largely by the National Bank and thereby outside the budget, has been an important factor.

The rise of forced intercompany credits has been a source of major distortions. As mentioned above, these are credits to companies that are temporarily or permanently unable to pay their bills (called "queuing" because the bills are arranged in a queue according to their due date). The amount of these forced credits is estimated to range currently between HF200 and HF400 billion. The latter amount is larger than the outstanding credits to the productive sector at the end of 1988. Compared with the amount of queuing, the continued net borrowing of households from the National Savings Bank has been a relatively minor problem.

As was stressed under "Controlling Inflation. . ." in Chapter 2, the future effectiveness of monetary policy is linked to the consolidation of not only companies, but also of the banking system. The commercial banks all have a large portfolio of bad debts on their balance sheets. Some of the debtors are paying interest, but in fact are unlikely to honor repayment obligations. The banks inherited a large portion of the bad debts and the bad debtors from the National Bank. (In fact, some of the claims on companies have been *de facto* subsidies and thus are part of the government's debts).

The capital base and the owned resources of the banks are also uncertain. In principle the banks were owned by the state, which had provided their original capital base. However, to enlarge their permanent resources, the banks have been allowed to sell shares to corporations, which in turn directly or indirectly are also owned by the state. It is difficult to see from the outside to what extent this situation represents a conflict of interest between owners, who are also actual or potential borrowers, and the banks, which are paying high dividends to their borrower-shareholders.

The rules on the use of the banks' resources appear to be quite elastic. Thus, banks are reported to have invested (heavily) in real estate (most of which is technically owned by the public sector) and to participate in complex privatization schemes.

There seem to be no effective restrictions on lending to *de facto* bankrupt companies as long as these companies are willing to pay interests (while neglecting to pay their other financial obligations). Banks appear not to have had interest to build up new accounts with the small new genuinely private companies trying to move out of the gray economy, in contrast to companies in the state sector that have enjoyed a *de facto* guarantee against bankruptcy and with joint-venture companies.

Hungary has a bankruptcy law, and lists are circulating about the companies that ought to go bankrupt. The previous government has also submitted to Parliament a list of the companies that have the largest negative positions. The principal criteria for becoming a candidate for potential bankruptcy are the size of the bad debts of the company in the queuing system, the extent of direct government subsidies, and their involvement in exports to nonconvertible currency markets. Yet, these criteria may not be economically rational ones, since the financial health of most enterprises was determined in the past (and is still influenced at present) by the complex system of financial attributions and withdrawals. The responsibility for inefficient management belongs to a large extent (although not exclusively) to the wrong signals coming from central political and economic decisions.

Company bankruptcies alone can solve neither the distortions in the banking and financial system nor the monetary shortcomings at the macroeconomic level. Also, because of the domino effect, "innocent" banks and companies (both suppliers and customers) could be rather hard hit in the absence of orderly bankruptcy procedures. At the same time, delaying bankruptcies tends to perpetuate financial, price, and market distortions and contributes to labor hoarding or de facto underemployment.

To expedite orderly bankruptcies, financial resources have to be set aside for an orderly procedure, and they have to be considered from the point of view of industrial reorganization (which must not be limited to seeking potential foreign investors).

THE LABOR MARKET

There is both labor shortage and hidden unemployment or underemployment in Hungary. Increased labor mobility, improved incentives, and better labor management are important aspects of the necessary structural change in Hungary. The number one priority is to increase the mobility of labor, both to increase the supply for new and growing companies and to reduce the wage bill for those that ought to cut their workforce to become more efficient.

The participation rate, although declining, remains relatively high at 45.7 percent. The share of the active population in agriculture is quite high at 20.5 percent of the total. According to official statistics, total employment has declined since 1980 by about 6 percent, essentially because of the aging of the population and a relatively early retirement age. These data may overstate the decline of the working population since many retired people remain employed at least on a part-time basis. At the same time, the official unemployment statistics (well below 1 percent of the active population) may also underestimate the actual unemployment or underemployment in various regions or population groups.

Since the 1970s, there have been two labor markets in Hungary, one of official jobs, and the other in the gray or parallel economy. Most people active in the gray economy have also kept an official job. People cling to their official jobs both because they were seen as an indirect unemployment insurance and because of the social benefits (and originally the obligations) connected with such jobs.

With few exceptions, productivity and work moral have been traditionally quite low in the official jobs, largely because of the lack of incentives (both positive and negative) and the inefficient organization of production. As a result, poor quality, lack of precision, and lack of respect for contractual deadlines have been endemic. Although most Hungarians are certainly overworked physically, it may be argued that one of the most devastating effects of the Socialist economy has been the corruption and demoralization in the official work place. This includes not only a high degree of absenteeism, but also a negligent and wasteful attitude toward customers, materials supplies, tools of production, stocks, and final products. It should also be pointed out that the volume and quality of the so-called "social services" connected with the jobs is quite low, and the working conditions (especially for workers in strenuous jobs) have deteriorated rather than improved. In recent years, liberalization on the one hand and creeping inflation on the other, have rather worsened this overall situation, in some cases leading to veritable pilferage and vandalism. The difference between the private and state-owned sectors (including the worker-managed companies) is striking in this respect.

General labor hoarding has been the traditional policy in the official job sector, in particular at the office level (in both the central bureaucracies and the productive sector). In the first place, this phenomenon has resulted from the lack of incentive for management (and for the workforce) to stimulate labor productivity and to have a lean but efficient staff. In fact numerous incentives in the system (including subsidies, investment quotas, and so forth) used to be linked, directly or indirectly, with the size of the workforce. Full (or near-full) employment has been also a social policy because of the lack of effective unemployment benefits and social safety network and because of the lack of reserves of most households that would allow them to cope with even relatively brief periods of unemployment (and the earlier legal obligation to have an official job to avoid the rather severe sanctions against vagrancy). The general tightness of the labor market and the difficulty of hiring labor as needed have led to classic labor-hoarding policies in most organizations. This situation has resulted in a low wage and productivity level in the official jobs sector.

The labor supply in the gray or parallel economy is composed to a sizeable extent of people who also have official jobs, thereby reducing the productivity of this segment of the labor market as well (except to the extent that they usually have access to tools and equipment in official jobs).

In fact, talk about the threat of increased unemployment (and the lack of effective social measures to cope with it) incites people to cling even more tightly to their official jobs and reduces labor mobility. It also makes it more difficult for new ventures to find qualified labor without having to offer expensive conditions or excessive wages. In the current situation, the practice of labor hoarding combined with low productivity and low wages has added to the twin problems of insufficient labor mobility and considerable wage pressures and wage inflation.

A Qualitative Change in the Reform Process

The success or failure of the current economic and political transformation will have a profound impact on the performance of the Hungarian economy in the years to come and on the country's chances of integration in the world economy.

There is considerable interest throughout the world in the success of the changes now taking place in Hungary and in its economic prosperity. Ever since the 1940s, it has been the explicit hope of the Western community of nations to see the peaceful transformation of the Eastern European countries into free and prosperous societies. The fact that profound changes are also taking place in the other Eastern European countries does not diminish the international interest in the transformation of the Hungarian economy. In fact, there is also a direct interest in the success of the Hungarian economy in Eastern Europe and in the Soviet Union. The parallel developments in the Eastern European countries could enhance the economic prospects of the area as a whole and improve the chances of success of each individual country. At the same time, it is also rightly believed that the economic and social prosperity of Hungary, as well as of the other Eastern European countries, could have a positive impact on the world economy.

For many years, Hungary was seen in both the East and the West as the most liberal, in economic and political terms, of the Socialist countries. This was recognized also by the Hungarian population, the OECD countries, and the international financial community.

The limits to political and economic reform, however, were also evident over the years both to outside observers and to Hungarian officials. Some of these limits were explicit, others implicit only. Some were imposed by the "internal logic of the system," others resulted from the personal choices of the Hungarian political leadership or of fears of Soviet disapproval. In the Socialist countries there was no clear division between political and economic decisions, between systemic problems and policy errors or arbitrary personal decisions. There was also considerable confusion between the need for improvements on the supply side and policies of demand management.

This situation was largely responsible for the checkered history of Hungarian economic reform since the 1960s. Despite the considerable achievements, it was obvious that the purely piecemeal approach, which was the only one politically possible, could not bring about the fundamental transformation of the economic order necessary for the sustained growth and prosperity of the Hungarian economy.

Since 1988 there has been a major qualitative change in the reform debate and in the official efforts to change the rules and structure of the Hungarian economy, turning away from the concept of a reformed Socialist economy, toward the model of a veritable market economy. The fall and winter of 1989–1990 have seen a marked acceleration of this trend. By late 1989 the goal of the creation of a free market economy was not only demanded by opposition economists, but it also became part of the election program of the ruling Socialist party (issued from the reformed Communist Party in October 1989) and of the legislative program of the government.

Today, the trial and error approach of reforming the system, while maintaining its fundamentally Socialist, planned character, is largely of historic interest only. For the first time in 40 years, not only can the need for a fundamental change of the very nature and objectives of the economy be openly discussed and advocated, but both the external and domestic political conditions for undertaking such an attempt appear to be realized. Yet, the structures and the functioning of the economy at the enterprise level have changed relatively little. In early 1990 there was a widespread feeling in the country that the power structure (or "power elite"), although more decentralized than at the beginning of the decade, had not yet been replaced.

The form of decentralization adopted a few years ago through the creation of employee and worker management councils is recognized today to have been a serious mistake. It gave too many rights to the people in place without submitting them to the risks and discipline of the market. The fact that about 75 percent of the companies (representing about 50 percent of production) became self-owned and self-managed entities, without any effective market and outside ownership control, has contributed to the perpetuation of structural rigidities and of distortions in the price and wage system. It has also been the source of real or alleged mismanagement of what is fundamentally public property, in the process of so-called "spontaneous privatization." The creation of the State Property Agency aims at correcting this earlier error, however as argued in the preceding chapter, this correction may not be sufficient. The management of a dual economy, where the Socialist and the monopolist enterprises and sectors predominate, will require a strong economic policy to provide the right incentives and exercising the right controls.

The magnitude and the technical complexity of the tasks ahead must not be underestimated. Sustained effort and sustained political consensus and support during the years to come is crucial. The bulk of the responsibility for this effort, and ultimately for the success or failure of the experiment, will belong to the Hungarians. At the same time, international cooperation (far beyond financial support) is extremely important. International economic cooperation has been a crucial element not only in the reconstruction of Western Europe after the war, but also in the unprecedented growth performance of the world economy during the last 40 years.

Major Legislative Developments

The increasingly charged legislative activity of the Hungarian government and Parliament since 1987, and especially in the fall and winter of 1989–1990, has contrasted sharply with the legislative calm of the preceding 40 years. It has aimed at defining the legal framework of the future market economy and at demonstrating within the country and abroad the fundamental and irreversible character of the break with the Communist political and economic model of society. Table I in the Appendix lists the 14 principal laws enacted during 1987, 1988, and 1989, and Table II lists the 55 other laws enacted during the same period.

It would be very difficult to summarize the 69 laws enacted in Hungary from 1987 through 1989, the legislation submitted to Parliament in January 1990, not to mention the many more regulations implementing these and earlier legislation. This is the expression of a veritable overload of the legislative process itself, especially in that 7 of the 14 principal legislative acts involve fundamental political change leading toward a democratic environment long enjoyed by OECD countries. Such legislation involves several amendments to the Constitution, establishing the freedoms of associations and of assembly, introducing the institution of popular referendum, and discontinuing the workers' militia.

Of the seven remaining principal laws, one deals with the reorganization of the country's banking structure; three with the introduction of taxation on personal and corporate incomes and of the VAT; one with corporations; one with the protection of foreign investments; and one with the transformation of corporations, state enterprises, and cooperatives from the public to the private sector. The general intent of the legislators in all these laws was to liberalize the country's economic structure and to create the basic framework for a market economy. In fact, the liberalization of economic policy has been less evident than the liberalization of the "ways and means" to it, and on a number of points it remains to be seen how well the apparently liberal intentions will translate into reality.

BANKING REFORM

The basic feature of the banking reform on January 1, 1987, was to devolve the normal commercial and investment banking functions to the private banking sector, created by the reform itself, from the Hungarian National Bank (HNB), which during the previous four decades enjoyed an almost complete monopoly over all banking activities. A significant exception during these 40 years was the National Savings Institution, also state owned, which handled almost all banking activities of private individuals, their liquid and savings deposits and their housing loans.

In the process of the banking reform, some 20 new banks were established, at least in part, by the partial transfer of assets and liabilities from the HNB. Four large banks predominate: the Hungarian Credit Bank, the Budapest Bank, the General Credit Bank, and the Bank of Foreign Commerce. These and the smaller banks then increased their capital by issuing stocks or bonds to other institutions and firms. As an example, the Hungarian Credit Bank has at present some 500 corporate stockholders and a share capital of some HF18 billion or $300 million. The number of banking institutions grew to about 30, where it stands at the present time. From January 1, 1990, the banks are expected to be authorized to handle limited foreign exchange transactions. It is also expected that the banks will reduce the nominal value of their shares so that private individuals might become stockholders.

The banks have been exposed to frequent criticism: their credit-policies are not quite clear, and their interest rates are high. This results mainly from the restrictive monetary policies of the HNB and from inflation, which makes it difficult to obtain liquid funds from the public. The most popular bond is a floating-rate issue, paying 1 percent more than inflation. The banks have invested in real estate, probably more heavily than desirable in view of the financing need of their clients. This, together with the factors mentioned earlier, has led to a serious liquidity squeeze.

The fast-changing economic and political climate created a tug-of-war among the government, the National Bank, and the mainly company-owned private banks (which in fact also belong to the state). Things previously forbidden became liberalized, and bank managers began to try to maximize their profits by using whatever methods seemed appropriate. The most popular was short-term loans without roll-over possibilities. Even today, banks have only a limited influence on policy making, and major contracts are still under strict National Bank control.

The bureaucracy within the banks is considerable. More than mere red tape, bank managers find it difficult to free themselves from old criteria of economic rationality or to distinguish between financial speculation and the promotion of the private economy. This is one of the reasons why many well meaning programs to assist small and medium-sized firms (such as those by World Bank and US/AID) are having trouble getting started.

Especially in the past, and to some extent in the present, it can be assumed that the small entrepreneur prefers cash to deposits for several reasons. Saving facilities were minimal. Banking activity was slow, the cashing of a cheque, even when it existed, took hours of queuing. To effect a regular transfer order might require (even now) a waiting period from several weeks to two months. Banking was not confidential; the local authorities were quite arbitrary in taxing small entrepreneurs, who in turn, tried to hide whatever income possible. Financial life seemed to have been loaded with distrust and suspicion on both sides, apart from legislative obstacles. Small entrepreneurs were considered second-class citizens. They felt they must pay high gratuities to suppliers and others to survive, which obviously could not appear on their books.

TAXATION

The purpose of the tax system introduced on January 1, 1988 and 1989, went beyond the obvious need to create revenue sources and the less obvious but not less pressing need to do away with the previous system of arbitrary levies and subsidies which for 40 years was the basis of public finances. Starting from the naive assumption that in socialism nobody has to pay taxes and no state enterprise need go broke, there was no income tax. The government transferred as often as necessary funds from state firms showing surpluses to state firms showing deficits. Since surpluses, by and large, were equal to deficits, the system actually worked for a while. There was a minuscule sector of private entrepreneurs (mostly small farmers and artisans) who were subject to taxes. However, as bank checks, even today, are not introduced to any meaningful extent, most payments were made in cash without records. Tax assessments were, under these circumstances, difficult, to say the least. No wonder that without personal and corporate income taxes and VAT, the rational management of a modern economy was impossible.

Personal income taxes were introduced on January 1, 1988. The maximum rate was 60 percent on the portion of incomes exceeding HF800,000. The minimum rate was 20 percent, on the portion of income between HF48,000 and HF70,000. The burden was therefore quite heavy on low income families. There have been minor changes in tax rates for 1989, and will be more for 1990, but not sufficiently great to make the system popular. The average rate for 1990 will be 14.5 percent of taxable incomes.

One of the main difficulties is the expense of collecting taxes. An even greater problem is that an estimated HF70 billion of personal incomes go unreported. The major offenders are doctors, small farmers, small entrepreneurs, barbers, taxi drivers, and so forth. The government seems to be unable or unwilling to face up to this issue seriously.

The method of introducing personal income taxes was quite ingenious. Employers, with government assistance, adjusted upwards employees' salaries on January 1, 1988, in such a manner that net, after-tax personal incomes remained virtually unchanged. In other words, during the first year the government subsidized the income taxes it received. This may have had a marked inflationary effect.

The VAT was introduced on January 1, 1988. For most items the rate is 25 percent, and for most services the rate is 15 percent. The total of 1988 VAT amounted to HF123 billion.

The Corporate Income Tax is not a new institution. However, because of the new Corporation Act and the Foreign Investment Act, which took effect on January 1, 1989, it was necessary to review previous statutes and to unify them in new legislation. The result is the new Corporate Profit Tax, which took effect on January 1, 1989. The corporate tax rate is 40 percent of taxable profit up to HF3 million, beyond which it is 50 percent. Some fields of activity are taxed at a lower rate. Further tax reduction is possible if the tax payer is a joint venture corporation with foreign participation of 20 percent or more. In 1990 corporate profit taxes will be reduced to 35 percent on incomes below HF3 million and 40 percent above it.

COMPANY AND OWNERSHIP REFORM

Undoubtedly, among the most important economic legislations of the period was the Corporation Act, the first omnibus legislation of its type in more than 100 years. The Act opens up the possibility of founding stock companies (with a minimum capital HF10 million), companies with limited responsibility (minimum capital HF1 million), joint ventures, and investment companies. At the application for incorporation, 30 percent of the capital, or at least HF5 million or HF0.5 million, respectively, must be paid in. Foreign investors can contribute up to 100 percent of the capital. If the foreign share is less than 50 percent, authorization follows almost automatically; if it is more, the waiting period is 90 days. The Company Registry Office might delay the procedure if it finds technical shortcomings in the application.

The Act on Foreign Corporations increases the assurances for foreign investors about repatriation of both capital and profits.

If the Corporation Act and the Act on Foreign Corporations unlocked the doors which might eventually lead to modern corporate activity, the Act on Transformation of Corporations made the next logical step in this direction. Whereas the Corporation Act is essentially directed at the formation and maintenance of new enterprises in the private sector, the Transformation Act focuses on the techniques to be used in the transformation of firms formerly in state or cooperative ownership into private corporations. Whereas the Corporation Act essentially promotes stability, the Transformation Act prescribes

ASSETS AND LIABILITIES

Principal Assets

1. Change from a traditional Socialist economy
2. Peaceful change of political and economic system towards market economy already well underway
3. Important human and labor resources with Western traditions and aspirations of success
4. Economy is functioning
5. Low wage levels and considerable productivity reserves
6. Geographic proximity to West and East
7. Strong consensus to rejoin community of European and Western nations
8. Dynamic parallel (private) economy
9. Small country with already high share of foreign trade
10. Considerable market and growth potential

Principal Liabilities

1. Loss of momentum of the economy and declining living standards
2. Large foreign debt and external and internal imbalances
3. Inefficient and run-down state industries and severe capital shortage in small private economy
4. Run-down and neglected infrastructure
5. Inheritance of piecemeal reform
6. Shortage of modern technology, products, and equipment
7. Large bureaucracy and inefficient management
8. Double-digit inflation, lack of motivation, and feeling of insecurity in large segments of population
9. Distorted foreign trade structure
10. Lack of experience in modern market economy

the way in which firms formerly in the public sector could enter the private sector. Its very duration is meant to be transitory, and it certainly does not aim to deal with major and long-term issues of property rights, ownership, and property management, which are subjects for separate legislations.

The conditions according to which firms can be transformed include the preparation of a plan of transformation, an audited balance sheet, and two consecutive announcements with at least a 15 days interval in the Official Register about the intended transformation. As discussed above, during 1984 and 1985, the state transferred its ownership right to the boards managing about 75 percent of individual enterprises, and has retained only a *de facto* veto in case of mismanagement. The ownership right includes the right to be transformed into enterprises in the private sector. Such transformation is normally initiated by the management of the corporation concerned, but the Council of Ministers could, in certain special cases, prevent transformation or veto it. Whatever portion of the capital that was in the ownership of the state at the time of transformation is to be transferred to the State Property Agency (SPA).

A further condition of the transformation is that the capital of the new firm should exceed the value of the old firm at least by 20 percent or HF100 million, whichever is larger. The purpose of this provision is to bring new capital, domestic and foreign, into the firm. The new firms can sell their stocks on the open market. As long as there is no SPA, its rights belong to the state organization, which originally created the firm, or to the Council of Ministers. The transformation procedure could be made more flexible through agreement between the firm and the SPA. The transformation of agricultural cooperatives should be regulated by the Law on Agricultural Cooperatives. Banks could be transformed into stock companies rather than into companies of limited responsibility.

Two new laws were adopted in early 1990 dealing with the management of state property and with the creation of a State Property Agency. This legislation is aimed at reducing some of the uncertainty and laxness involved in the management of state-owned enterprises and in the "spontaneous" privatization process. As with earlier legislation they, too, will need clarification and strengthening to achieve transparency and order in this complex and vital area.

Major Tasks Ahead

In the years ahead Hungary will need an effective government, and an effective Parliament, with broad popular support. They will have to agree on a long-term program for the Hungarian economy. The "grand design" required is not that of the one-party state. It is rather the kind of consensus that exists among the various political parties in the Continental European countries, the United States or Japan, about the fundamental values, characteristics, and objectives of society.

The first Parliament elected through free elections in the Spring of 1990 has a particularly complex task. It will have to review old and newer legislation to check its compatibility with a free society and a market economy and adopt additional or corrective measures aimed at completing the peaceful and efficient transformation of the Hungarian economy. At the same time, it will have to be mindful of the need to avoid the danger of an "overproduction" of new laws and regulations and of too frequent changes in rules, which

PRINCIPAL RECOMMENDATIONS—
AN AGENDA FOR ACTION
   I.   Clear framework of long-term economic and social goals and policies
  II.   Task Force Hungary, an integrated task force of Western and Hungarian officials
 III.   Hungarian-International Long-Term Credit and Development Bank
  IV.   Comprehensive long-term debt-adjustment program
   V.   Control of inflation, competition, and private property, and an effective reform of the monetary, banking, and financial systems

The Tasks Ahead
1. Implement the main recommendations
2. A program for sustained, balanced, and equitable economic growth
3. Promoting economic freedom and increased incentives for private initiative
4. Promoting structural and technological change
5. Competition, prices and waste reduction
6. Restoring the sense of responsibility throughout the economy
7. A more limited and more efficient state
8. Increasing labor mobility and productivity
9. An active social policy and effective unemployment insurance
10. Labor peace
11. Promoting savings and private ownership
12. Restoring effective ownership control
13. A stable national currency
14. Integration with the European and world economies
15. Democratic control and transparent budget practices
16. Careful management of external resources
17. An effective industrial policy
18. Infrastructure and effective protection of the environment
19. Housing policy
20. Personnel training

would create confusion and would interfere with the development of the private economy.

The need for stability must be stressed. There is an inevitable aspect of trial and error in all economic policies. This will be all the more true during the coming period of transformation and transition. Because of this, it is important to break the habits of continually tinkering with economic rules and structures, of poorly thought through decisions and reforms that had to be corrected or reversed shortly after introduction. A legal vacuum, or constantly changing rules and laws, can hamper economic activity and raise costs as much as overregulated economy. Tinkering with economic directives or legislation is an expensive and dangerous temptation in a market economy; many parliamentary democracies routinely succumb to this temptation. The importance of maintaining law and order in the economy, as in the society at large, during the complex years of transition will test the skills and resolve of the new government.

This section contains a list of major tasks facing Hungary in the 1990s. They include the Agenda for Action based on the five most urgent recommendations described in the previous chapter. The list sums up the principal issues to be addressed in Hungary, beyond the short-term management of the economy, to avoid a financial and social breakdown; several are of a longer term or structural character. However, all have to be addressed from the start to reverse the current stagnation and drift of the economy into a firm direction and to create a consistent platform for a sustained growth.

As stated earlier in establishing this list of issues, originality was not the primary motivation. In fact, it is encouraging how much common ground exists between the perception of the issues and priorities by an outside group of experts and the sense of urgency many Hungarians feel about their tasks for the future.

■ The Five Main Recommendations

The five main recommendations, defined in the preceding chapter, are the core of an Agenda for Action. Their implementation would facilitate progress on most of the other issues and tasks on the Agenda. They can be simply mentioned here without detailed comment, since they were described at length in Chapter 2.

- A *"grand design" for balanced growth, international economic integration, and the development of a modern market economy in Hungary.*
  It is argued in this report that such a "grand design" could find inspiration in the successful experience of the Western European economies during the postwar period and their common tradition of the social market economy.

- A *joint task force of officials from Hungary and the OECD countries to promote Hungary's integration into the world economy.*
  Such a temporary task force could help focus and coordinate the cooperation with, and assistance to, Hungary during the crucial period of transition over the next two to three years.

- *A Hungarian-International Long-Term Credit and Development Bank for the optimum utilization of resource transfer.*

   This bank could play a key role in assuring the efficient use of the resource transfer to Hungary and in major development tasks (e.g., private enterprises, productive infrastructure, environmental protection).

- *A negotiated long-term debt-adjustment program.*

   Debt adjustment is vital for the successful development of the Hungarian economy, and thus it is in the interest also of Hungary's foreign creditors. To have a lasting, positive impact, such a plan will have to be part of a comprehensive program of the kind described in other recommendations.

- *Controlling inflation, promoting private property and competition, and completing the reform of the National Bank.*

   Developing a credible, long-term anti-inflationary program is an urgent task. It has to include not only liberalization and competition, but also an effective wage and price policy. It is necessary to promote the development of private initiative and private property; it is equally necessary to assure the efficient management of the numerous state-owned companies. These tasks are closely connected with the effective autonomy of the central bank and the consolidation of the banking system.

2 A Program for Sustained, Balanced, and Equitable Economic Growth

Creating the basis for a sustained, balanced, and equitable growth has to be the top long-term objective of Hungarian economic policy. This is an economic, political, and social priority. It is as necessary for easing the difficulties inherent in the fundamental changes to come as it is for restoring the external financial position of Hungary. Continued economic stagnation would discredit the idea of the market economy and endanger the social acceptance of economic freedom and responsibility.

Economic austerity as such is neither an acceptable social goal nor a workable economic program. Austerity is defensive. It implies the more or less arbitrary sharing of shortages or poverty by nonmarket restrictions. It undermines incentives and discourages effort, thus ultimately limiting productivity improvements and higher output. In most cases so-called austerity policies have achieved neither lasting domestic nor sustainable external equilibrium. This was the case in postwar Britain and more recently during the 1980s in the heavily indebted Latin American countries.

The fundamental criticism of austerity is that it is wasteful. It wastes potential efforts and output, but does not necessarily eliminate the waste of resources in the economy.

Continuing wealth creation, and not wealth distribution, is the principal feature of successful economies. Thus, sustained economic growth and the rise in individual and collective living standards associated with it (increasing incomes, savings, and consumption) have to be the central objectives of Hungarian economic policy. Economic growth, however, cannot be sustained without macroeconomic, domestic as well as external equilibrium. Balance does not equate with austerity, which is neither a social goal nor an economic program. The effective search for productive macroeconomic equilibrium rests on the efficient use of the scarce resources of the Hungarian economy.

3 Promoting Economic Freedom and Increased Incentives for Private Initiative

The principal economic resource of Hungary is its population. It is also the most ill-used and wasted resource in the economy. Until recently, many people still did not believe in the reality of economic freedom in Hungary today. Many impediments to initiative remained for ordinary people, households, and would-be entrepreneurs.

Yet freeing the productive energies of the Hungarian population is the principal microeconomic requirement for economic growth. The macroeconomic goals, neither growth and rising living standards nor foreign and domestic balance, can be achieved without an upsurge in private initiative, productivity, and individual interest and responsibility at all levels in the economy. This objective requires a drastic reduction in bureaucracy and red tape. There is a need to strengthen the commercial culture. Raw material and production prices must reflect real scarcities. People have to believe that it is worth taking the initiative and working more efficiently. They have to become aware of the existence of market-conforming positive and negative incentives, true economic rewards, and sanctions.

Economic freedom is an essential counterpart of political freedom and autonomy. After 40 years during which private initiative was at best part of the gray economy and private companies had virtually no capital, it is important to demonstrate the reality of economic freedom. Thus, special measures to encourage private initiative and the accumulation of capital by the new, small and medium-sized companies ought to have a high priority in the years to come. The proposed Hungarian-International Bank could play a useful role, along with numerous other private and public initiatives. Economic freedom, however, is important not only for entrepreneurs, but also for workers, employees, and obviously for consumers.

The whole philosophy of economics, the role of the state, and the approach to enterprise and wealth creation must also change. The change in thinking has to permeate all official bodies as well as universities and schools, and the people who work in them. The intellectual constraints and ideological resistance that have obstructed free economic initiative must go. In other words a change must be brought about in the way people think. For over 40 years public thought has been dictated by the party and by the state. Virtually everything has been done from the viewpoint of the state, not the individual. The telescope must be turned around. This needed change in the way people—including economists, bureaucrats, managers, educators, and workers—think will be a long-term process. In many cases institutional change will be a prerequisite. These profound changes in thinking cannot be imposed from outside. They have to come from within the country and be voiced by a convinced leadership.

Privilege and power always oppose change. Incentives can be provided to small-scale entrepreneurs who are already doing their best to improve their lot, but they cannot easily be provided to bureaucrats. A system of incentives and rewards for changed attitudes must be put into place to promote a new spirit of enterprise. Citizens must be encouraged to take initiatives and risks. They must be shown that making money and acquiring wealth are laudable aims, and that the wealthy individual can provide benefits to the community of a kind that are or should be outside the scope of the state and the bureaucracy to provide.

4 Promoting Structural and Technological Change

Structural changes, rather than resource transfers from abroad, have to be seen as the principal source of growth in the 1990s for the Hungarian economy. In fact, the main objective of resource transfer ought to be to promote these changes and to channel them in the most productive direction. There is a great need and a very broad scope of gradual structural changes throughout the economy. These structural changes will result from a combination of

- Systemic changes and a more competitive, more rational, and more favorable economic environment

- More efficient behavior at the level of existing enterprises and the introduction of new technologies and modern management techniques

- Creation and growth of new enterprises, including the current gray economy, and the expansion of a truly private, market economy, including Hungarian-owned, foreign-owned, and joint ventures.

This will involve important technological changes at all levels of the economy. Beyond buying new machinery, introducing computers, or automating, it means a different attitude and a different organization in industry, services, and agriculture. Technological change could be as significant for improved living standards in Hungary as it has been in the OECD countries and in the rapidly growing economies of the Far East.

Technological change is not the same as capital formation, although they are often linked in discussion. The two processes are quite distinct. Introduction of new technology usually requires some investment, but the significance of technological change is quite unrelated to the amount of investment associated with it. Much technological change draws very little on the supply of savings; indeed, technological change often saves capital. The use of computers reduces the stock of raw materials and components required to sustain a given flow of final output. The savings in working capital can far exceed the cost of the computers. The economies of the West have experienced exceptionally rapid technological changes, which have reached Hungary in only an attenuated form. The use of computers, FAX machines, and sophisticated methods of stock control are obvious examples. To benefit from these changes requires a modernization of the mind.

The Hungarian government will have to pursue an active and imaginative technology policy at several levels: by revising the organization of R&D support, by encouraging the diffusion of modern technologies throughout the economy, by promoting the development of Hungarian technologies (without, however, committing the error of technology nationalism or protectionism), and through technology imports, including buying licenses, technology transfer, purchasing state-of-the-art equipment. Technology can be related to product design and to the production process. Modern technologies are not limited to "high-tech."

In general the contribution of direct foreign investments is likely to be greater through the technology brought in by the foreign companies than through their complementing Hungarian savings and the country's financial resources.

5 Competition, Prices, and Waste Reduction

Hungary has already embarked on a bold price reform. Hungarian officials are fully aware that it is not enough to liberalize prices. It is also important to prevent abusive (monopolistic or oligopolistic) price behavior that could jeopardize the success of the price reform. The necessary task of eliminating the principal price distortions in CMEA has also begun.

The objective is to have a market-conforming price structure. This does not imply the same relative prices for all assets, goods, and services as in the OECD countries (among those are also important differences). It is essential, however, to have internationally competitive prices for tradable goods and services.

An essential condition of a return to economic growth and of the long-term success of economic reform is the reduction of waste throughout the economy. This is not a matter of police control and anti-waste campaigns, but of economic and business management and of incentives, both positive and negative. It can be achieved only through competitive pricing.

In the last 40 years wasteful economic management became a way of life in Communist economies. If the Hungarian economy was somewhat better off in this respect than others, the urgency of reversing this situation must not be underestimated. The most striking manifestation of this is the wasteful use of labor. Wasteful management has also characterized the use of foreign exchange and other external resources, as well as of raw materials, machinery, and the infrastructure. Most recently people are expressing legitimate concern that the same wasteful approach is being applied to state property and to the country's scarce capital stock.

The last ten years have seen a loss of substance in the country's capital stock. The efficient, market-conforming use of investment funds is essential to reducing waste in Hungary.

Standards of living are very low compared with Western Europe, and it will take a long time to catch up. It can be done, however, not through Western subsidies, but through Hungarian wealth creation. The incentives and rewards for anyone with entrepreneurial skills must encourage hard work, long working hours, and high levels of domestic savings and investment. Investment must take priority over consumption and be focused on productive enterprise.

Productive capital formation can be a potent instrument of economic progress. Accordingly, domestic savings and the provision of investable funds from abroad can contribute significantly to such advancement. These matters are occasionally overemphasized in the discussions on Hungarian economic reform. Spending does not become productive simply by calling it investment, in the sense of monetary spending other than on consumption. The quality of investment is critically important. Investment is productive only if, over the lifetime of the asset, it increases output more than its cost, including interest and amortization. The productivity of investment should not be taken for granted. This applies conspicuously to the contemporary Third World and to the Socialist economies in which investable funds have been wasted on a massive scale.

Even when capital formation is productive, it is usually not a critical element in economic advancement. In the progress of the West over the last two centuries, other factors have been quantitatively more important, including changes in attitudes, redeployment of resources, and technological advance. Because these changes do not absorb resources in the way investment does, they permit an improvement of current living standards, which in turn serves as inducement for improved economic performance. The need to find resources for investment, especially when it comes from increased taxation, can serve as a disincentive to effort and enterprise, which can offset or exceed the benefits from the investment.

▦ 6 Restoring the Sense of Responsibility Throughout the Economy

Socialism has greatly diminished the sense of responsibility throughout the Hungarian economy. This has been more a systemic problem than a sign of character or moral decay. For four decades people have been living under a double standard. The widespread condoning of careless or even irresponsible ways of dealing with state property have contrasted sharply with the traditional moral standards in the personal or private sphere. One of the fundamental advantages of the market economy is that its dynamic rewards and sanctions encourage economically responsible behavior. Responsibility is the direct corollary of freedom: this is true in the political as well as in the economic sphere. A free economy, even more than a market economy, depends on stable and transparent rules of behavior. The market rewards productive activity and sanctions uneconomic activity. The market economy is not the jungle: there is also loyalty to a firm and commitment by the firm to the welfare of its workers and employees. In a free economy people know that their work and success will be rewarded by the market, but only economic activities that are found useful by others (i.e., by the community) are rewarded by the market. Where the market does not, or does not yet, apply effective sanctions, other forms of control have to be introduced or reinforced. The fight against corruption and the abuse of economic power, however, should not be misdirected against market competition.

▦ 7 A More Limited and More Efficient State

The economic role of the state will have to become more limited, and the weight of politics in economic decisions will have to diminish. This also explains the need for an autonomous central bank outside the reach of the day-to-day political control of the government or Parliament.

At the same time, the efficiency of the state and the respect for the state will have to increase. Not only because Hungary is likely to remain, for many years to come, a mixed economy, and the state must not abdicate the final responsibility for the efficient management of the capital for which it acts as custodian. In all the successful modern economies, even where the government, as in Switzerland, does not own or operate production companies, the state has important functions at all levels (municipal, regional, and national) in creating favorable conditions for the efficient operation of the economy (*Rahmenbedingungen* in German or *conditions cadre* in French). The state must not only ensure competition and market-conforming behavior (and control the abusive exercise of private or public concentrations of economic power), but also protect the interests of the collectivity rather than the vested interests in the private or the public sector.

The state, in its political, economic, and social functions, has been deeply discredited in Hungary, as in many other Socialist countries. Defining clearly the future role of the state in the economy and increasing the efficiency of government action and administration are key requirements for the future success of the Hungarian economy. Increasing the efficiency of the state (which does not mean increasing its weight) is not something that can be postponed; it must be attended to during the more or less protracted period of transition in the years ahead.

An important task will be, for example, to provide support for the private sector by making those infrastructural improvements that will facilitate a higher rate of return from private sector activity. State activities that do not contribute to wealth creation should be kept to a level compatible, however, with welfare, justice and humanitarian considerations.

A timetable for trimming the bureaucracy should be established that encompasses the whole concept of organization. Thus, for example, numerous engineers and researchers may have to move from largely administrative positions to jobs more closely linked to business and production.

Even if movement between jobs, activities, and places is encouraged, some people will be unavoidably hurt by the proposed economic reforms. On both humanitarian and political grounds, much thought must be given how the hardest hit could be compensated, whether in money or by reassignment to other tasks and possibly by maintenance of their status. This will undoubtedly pose major problems. Unless the government makes clear that the financial position, living conditions, and perhaps even status of those threatened by the reforms will be protected, the political and social opposition may prove insurmountable. Such considerations strengthen the case for gradualism in the introduction of some of the major changes.

8 Increasing Labor Mobility and Productivity

People are the most important resource of Hungary: motivating them and freeing their productive energies and imagination are among the most important tasks of political leadership and of economic policy. The labor market will be key to the success or failure of the Hungarian economy in the years ahead. Today, Hungary suffers both from a shortage of motivated and productive labor and from hidden underemployment. Many people are badly overworked, while others (sometimes even highly trained scientists and engineers) are being paid to stay within the organization. One of the most immediate tasks of deregulation and of the introduction of free markets is to eliminate waste and to bring about a more productive and more efficient use of existing labor resources.

Companies need clear economic and financial disincentives for labor hoarding. Individuals should not benefit from clinging to unproductive jobs: there should be clear incentives for them to accept mobility, changing jobs and status, and even temporary unemployment.

In order to increase motivations and productivity, a true (nonautomatic) bonus system ought to be tested (and should receive favorable tax treatment). Under such systems, which are widely used in Japan and other countries, the level of bonuses (which can amount to substantial yearly or half-yearly payments) are directly linked to the company's overall performance. These systems also help stimulate savings over consumption.

There is widespread anxiety in the country about the scope and outcome of the reforms. Many people are deeply worried about how they will be affected. This is understandable: some party functionaries, managers, and workers in state enterprises will lose their jobs, consumers will be hit by higher prices, and tenants will be affected by housing reforms. This is, of course, a major reason why economic reform is so much more difficult than political reform. Certain conclusions—economic, social, humanitarian, and political—follow from this.

Making it easier for people to move between activities and places could reduce the hardship for those who have been displaced from their former activity. Such movement is inhibited in a closely regulated economy. In Hungary much economic activity is still confined to the state and other public authorities. Moreover, as mentioned above, there are also restrictions of various kinds in setting up enterprises even in the private sector. The more these obstacles to movement are removed, the easier it will be for displaced people to be absorbed in productive activity, and the less they will have to fear being displaced.

Easier movement between activities must be accompanied by easier movement between places. This is closely related to housing reform. It is required not only to prevent further deterioration of the housing stock, but also to facilitate movement between places and therefore between jobs. The exclusive promotion of owner-occupied housing may not be the right solution. In all housing markets there is a need for a mix of apartments and houses to buy and rent. An increase in company housing or company housing loans could also help.

Removing some of the social benefits connected with having an official job from the responsibility of the work place would also facilitate mobility. These benefits would not add to public sector expenses, partly because they represent future payments and partly because they would allow reduced subsidies and other government expenses, including wages and salaries of those who will be taken off the government's payroll. Financial incentives for those willing to leave their jobs ought to be applied more systematically. Finally, it is important to introduce effective incentive schemes (most of the previous incentive schemes were eliminated with the introduction of the income tax).

9 An Active Social Policy and Effective Unemployment Insurance

An effective economic policy is not conceivable without a well thought out and effective social policy. Such a social policy must have two central objectives: to promote the market economy by encouraging mobility and risk-taking and to help those who will be hurt by the changes in the economic system and the increased competition in the economy. Because of low real incomes and reserves, an economic policy aimed at increased labor mobility and at labor shedding will not work without an effective unemployment policy. (To accept the principle of caring for the truly needy, it is also important to prevent the creation of large groups of professional unemployed, who abuse the system and find work in the gray economy.) The costs of this policy have to be carried by the economy as a whole. The objective is not a redistribution of income, but help to the needy and preventing the pauperization of certain segments of society.

Providing efficient and decent social services for those who need them, including those who will be the most affected by the transition to a new economic order, will be all the more important since, now and in the foreseeable future, most Hungarian companies can provide little effective social services and insurance (except for the dubious service of labor hoarding).

Assuming these tasks should not be incompatible with the necessity to reduce taxes and the government's say in the distribution of income. The British economist Colin Clark, while arguing in favor of a limit on taxation and income redistribution, had the following to say about the need for social policies:

> A government which ignores social justice comes under the terrible condemnation of Saint Augustine—*remota justitia quid sunt regna nisi magna latrocinia*—"a government which has departed from justice is nothing but large-scale gangsterism." Social justice means respecting the right of groups. It certainly does not mean an attempt to create equality, or the transfer of income from one section to another by arbitrary decision, or legislation conferring special favors on any section. It is, however, the right and duty of the state to use public funds to relieve real need, when it cannot be relieved otherwise. This concept should be broadly defined. "By necessities as I understand not only the commodities which are necessary for the support of life," wrote Adam Smith, "but whatever the custom of the country renders it indecent for creditable people, even at the lowest order, to be without." [*The State of Taxation*, Institute of Economic Affairs, London, 1977, p. 25]

10 Labor Peace

Peaceful and constructive labor-management relations are also an essential element of the future success of the Hungarian economy. The achievement of this objective depends on economic and political leadership (and on the organization of labor-management relations) and on the incentives for labor to adopt a cooperative stance. The constructive attitude of labor (i.e., no disruptive labor practices and the acceptance of the measures to stimulate productivity) has been essential for the growth and prosperity of the major continental European economies from reconstruction throughout the postwar period. Germany, Austria, Switzerland, and numerous other countries have shown that it does not take massive unemployment or an authoritarian regime to secure social peace and basically rational labor behavior. At the same time, the example of the United Kingdom has shown that the responsibility for disruptive labor actions during several decades did not belong only to labor, but was shared by unimaginative management attitudes and the lack of social consensus in the factories and in the economy.

Putting the burden of adjustment on the prices of basic goods and services is not conducive to labor peace. Adam Smith argued in 1776 that "whatever raises this average price [of the necessary articles of subsistence] must necessarily raise those wages...." [*The Wealth of Nations*, The Modern Library, New York, p. 822]

11 Promoting Savings and Private Ownership

The issue of savings has been raised earlier. Encouraging private ownership and protecting private savings are major dimensions of social policy in a market economy. Higher household savings are essential for stimulating economic growth and modernization of the Hungarian economy. These savings, however, should not take the form of forced savings, i.e., of inflation and/or rising levels of taxation. Nor should savings lead to capital flight (or of flight into foreign currencies). The main preconditions for stimulating savings are reliable safeguards for private ownership and savings, a stable domestic currency, letting corporate profits rise, a positive return of savings, and new instruments of savings.

As in many other countries, housing has been the most effective means of promoting savings in Hungary. In the future this should remain a major, but not the only, outlet for savings.

Both for social and economic reasons, the gradual program of privatization should be connected with broadening share-ownership. As mentioned before, the objective is not to create worker-controlled managements (in fact, some of the shares may be of the nonvoting kind) nor to assure an initial flow of dividend income to the shareholders. However, broad segments of the Hungarian population should have the opportunity to own shares in Hungarian companies, and to benefit from the likely appreciation in the long run of productive assets.

12 Restoring Effective Ownership Control

A firm and clear recognition of property rights is of the utmost importance. Effective deployment and management of assets requires close connection between ownership and control. Assets will be used most effectively if their ultimate owners exercise control, are assured of the rewards, and bear the cost of failure. Saving and enterprise require that their fruits will not be confiscated. This applies particularly in a country where within one adult lifetime, many thousands of people, rich and poor, have lost their possessions through political action, including real property, business assets, personal belongings, and savings. People's confidence is understandably rather fragile.

Inflation and large-scale, abusive asset stripping will discredit the budding market economy in Hungary more quickly and certainly than anything else. The reportedly careless way of dealing with the public's property is one of the most evident vestiges of the wasteful management of the Socialist economy.

To create an economy in which private property will play an important role, respect for private property has to be developed. A first aspect of this respect is that it will not be expropriated, whether directly through nationalization or indirectly through open or repressed inflation. An equally important dimension of this respect is to ensure that property can be acquired and conserved only through "honest" means, i.e., through savings, economic success, or inheritance. The poorer the economy and the more fragile the notion of private property, the more important it is that the acquisition of property should be above suspicion.

The two major drawbacks of pervasive state ownership in Hungary have been that it leads to and/or reinforces a misallocation of resources in the economy and that, because of its impersonal nature and people's doubts about the legitimacy of state ownership, it leads to a careless management of state property.

The disposal of state property to anyone who happens to be there (which, in fact, is a system of spoils) would seriously jeopardize the future of the Hungarian market economy. It would perpetuate a tradition of wasteful and careless business management in the Hungarian economy, undermine respect for private property, and create the impression that corruption is an easier way to property acquisition than saving and market success.

13 Stabilizing the National Currency

The fastest way to destroy an economy is by debasing or corrupting its currency. A sound currency is a precondition for sustained and socially equitable economic growth. A stable national currency ought to be a fundamental goal in Hungary; it is necessary to eliminate foreign and domestic price distortions and the subsiding of excessive wage pressures. It is illusory and dangerous to believe that the role of a stable national currency could be assumed by a foreign or parallel currency (e.g., the dollar or the German mark). The first aspect of stability to pursue is the domestic purchasing power of the forint; domestic stability is the precondition of external stability and convertibility. In terms of its external value, an undervaluation of the forint ought to be avoided, as well as an overvaluation that would undermine the international competitive position of Hungarian products and services.

Further progress toward convertibility is an essential requirement of modernization and economic growth. However, it would be dangerous to assume that a reasonable (market) exchange rate could be achieved through immediate full convertibility before domestic prices are more in line with world market prices and excess domestic demand has been greatly reduced. As for general exchange rate policy, shadowing the ECU seems reasonable from the point of view of both domestic stability and Hungarian foreign trade. In the long run, with the desired improvement of the competitive position of the Hungarian economy, a rise in the exchange rate, and an improvement in the terms of trade could be expected.

All this is a restatement of the points under the fifth set of recommendations in Chapter 2 in favor of the absolute need to assure the effective autonomy of the Hungarian National Bank by endowing it with policy tools that are not neutralized by various pressure groups or leakages in the system.

The statistics available for, and from, the National Bank have to be improved. Timely and precise information should be made available about its objectives and policies. There ought to be close cooperation with the BIS and various OECD central banks. The central bank working group of Task Force Hungary could help strengthen the existing contacts and assume an important role during the reform of the National Bank and the transition phase.

14 Integration with the European and World Economy

The adoption of a coherent, liberal external economic policy is also a precondition for the transformation, growth, and modernization of the Hungarian economy. The liberalization of trade and broadening convertibility are necessary to strengthen the competitive position of the Hungarian economy through increased freedom and competitive pressures.

One of the main advantages of international economic integration is that it imposes an external discipline not only on individual companies but also on macroeconomic management. To the extent that Hungarian producers need temporary protection, tariffs are less harmful to the general interest than quantitative restrictions. However, both effective trade liberalization and even limited (current account) convertibility presuppose the elimination of domestic excess demand and effective macroeconomic management.

Hungary is in the fortunate position of being a relatively small country. Generally, small economies have fared as well or better than large ones in the postwar period because of their greater flexibility and openness toward outside influence. Also, the share of exports and imports in total output and expenditure is already quite large in Hungary. Hungary ought to follow, directly or indirectly, a policy of export-led growth or dynamic output specialization or adaptation. In addition to an export-friendly macroeconomic stance, this will require considerable improvement in quality and market adequacy: a continuous adjustment to demand via market sensitivity, education and research, active market observation and research, flexible production, and a very strong emphasis on quality control.

The promotion of foreign direct investments and technology imports in Hungary ought to aim at the qualitative improvement and integration into Western production and marketing networks. A gradual integration with the European and the world economy will open new markets and raise competitive pressures ("discipline") at both the macroeconomic level and at the company level. In the short run, the reality of the progress of integration is more important than its institutional form (and the reduction or elimination of various forms of discrimination and trade restrictions by the OECD countries are a very positive development); the long-term objective of institutional integration ought to be part of the "grand design" from the start.

The problems related to CMEA trade (distorted price structure and dependence on export markets, energy, and raw materials supplies) ought to be handled with determination, but gradually. Neither the objective nor the outcome should be a drastic reduction of Hungarian trade with the Soviet Union and other Eastern European countries. The pressure for better quality (and thus more favorable prices) ought to be applied with equal rigour to Eastern and Western trade. The issue of the security of Hungary's energy supplies ought to be one of the topics to be dealt with by Task Force Hungary.

15 Democratic Control and Transparent Budget Practices

There are various ways of counting the government share in the national income. Whatever the approach, the share of the GDP over which the government has control ought to be diminished in Hungary in the future. (In the OECD countries the public sector controls between 30 and 55 percent of the national revenue in the form of direct expenditures and transfer payments, compared with nearly 70 percent in Hungary.)

One of the immediate tasks is to draw a much clearer distinction between, on the one hand, the state budget and the budget of regional and local authorities, and on the other hand, the numerous state-owned and state-run companies. This is important not only for the currently autonomous companies, but for virtually all the state-owned sector. It is also important to increase the transparency and the control over the numerous special funds.

The goal is not to eliminate immediately all subsidies or all deficits, although the reduction of subsidies is an important task. Most market-oriented economies there are subsidized sectors and companies (housing and agriculture, in particular) as well as occasional deficits. The objective is to bring greater economic rationality and political accountability into public finance, which will accommodate the resources and priorities of the Hungarian economy. Among the most important tasks of the elected representatives of the people is to decide about the level of the government budget, the priorities as well as the control of the spending of public funds. Thus, three urgent tasks have to be accomplished:

- Define the nature of government action and the priorities of government spending

- Project a sound balance of revenues and expenditures in macroeconomic terms (domestic and external monetary stability, economic growth, financial equilibrium)

- Establish effective supervision, control, and responsibilities with regard to the execution of the approved government budget.

Geographic decentralization of the government budget may be an important political objective. It is, however, less important than a rigorous implementation of these tasks. In fact, decentralization must not be used for circumventing the budgetary priorities or controls.

16 Careful Management of External Resources

The potential contribution of capital imports to the growth and modernization of the Hungarian economy is rightly emphasized in Hungary and abroad. It was argued in the preceding chapter that the main problem was not the size of past capital imports, but the use to which they had been put. Although past or present policy errors must not be taken lightly, it is important to realize that without measures of the kind suggested in this report, Hungary could be forced to repeat, in the not too distant future, some of the serious errors of its past. The problem is not the danger of a lack of availability of external financial resources, but the terms and conditions on which these resources are made available, and even more importantly, the use which is made of them.

In principle there will be considerable scope for profitable productive investment in Hungary should be broadened in the years to come. As for the sources of funds, one avenue might follow the suggestion that various European countries could relax restrictions on the investments that insurance companies and pension funds are permitted to hold to increase the inflow of productive funds without significant risk to the insurance companies or pension funds.

Because of the importance of this issue, some basic principles discussed earlier may be repeated here. Foreign direct investments should be encouraged, but accompanied by certain rules to protect Hungarian interests. In the case of large takeovers, the government may consider reserving small minority holdings such as "golden shares" and first option in case of resale. As far as possible, capital imports or the transfer of resources should not be debt-creating. To avoid inflationary consequences from capital imports, part of the forint counterpart might be sterilized or frozen. Receipts from the sale of assets should not be used to finance deficits or current spending, and financing the government deficit by foreign borrowing should cease immediately. The real rate of return in Hungary ought to be as high or higher than the cost of foreign capital. Certain low-return, for example infrastructural, projects ought to be financed if possible on concessionary terms, or the difference in return from current receipts.

17 An Effective Industrial Policy

Most OECD countries have adopted industrial policies as well as agricultural and energy policies. Despite, or because of, past experience with central economic planning, Hungary needs an effective industrial policy that includes the agriculture and services sectors. Industrial policy does not mean charting a detailed course for the development of domestic firms or providing permanent subsidies or protection for them. The costs of so-called "infant industry" policies are often much higher than the benefits. Nevertheless, Hungary could benefit from the broad range of positive or negative policy experiences in Western Europe and the other OECD countries.

As stressed throughout the present study, the most pressing task is achieving a more effective management of state-owned companies. This will require incentives, sanctions, controls and more efficient management methods.

A plan to reorganize or close inefficient companies and to implement a gradual privatization of state-owned companies is also needed. The government must reaffirm its ownership rights and control over the self-owned companies, which had been virtually given away to the management and workers by the state under the ill-inspired reform mentioned above. By now, it is obvious that the Yugoslav model of worker management leads neither to democracy nor to the market economy; it is a recipe for economic disorder.

The following measures might also be included in Hungarian industrial policies:

- Promote the development of designs, norms, and standards compatible with European and worldwide norms

- Promote rigorous quality standards and fair commercial practices, and introduce a credible quality label

- Stimulate competition and an open market for highly qualified personnel by increasing wage and salary differentials. (It is important to avoid a brain-drain from state-owned companies and from Hungary generally, and it should also be possible to attract specialized foreign personnel to state-owned companies, and not only in joint ventures and consulting bureaus)

- Create new industrial zones and high-tech areas for Hungarian companies and foreign export-oriented companies

- Increase the compatibility of basic systems, such as energy distribution, transportation, and communications, with European systems

- Develop centers for advanced services, and improve the availability of various services (information, export promotion) needed by small and medium-sized companies

- Create official trouble-shooting services for utilities, housing, legal problems, labor, etc. to facilitate the start-up of both foreign and domestic companies

- Improve accounting standards and the quality and volume of industrial and company information

- Actively promote supplier relationships with multinational industrial and commercial companies

- Develop an active technology policy.

As for agriculture, it should be sufficient to say here that Hungary needs a farm policy that will allow it to maintain and improve the volume and quality of the supply to its domestic market and to maintain, at least for the foreseeable future, its export capacity. It would be unfortunate indeed if, as a result of policy changes, shortages appeared on the domestic market (instead of more plentiful and higher quality supplies), and if Hungary were to lose some of its export markets in the CMEA countries and elsewhere. Property and structural reform in farming should be driven by higher productivity, increased competition, and improved quality, rather than by political expediency.

18 Infrastructure and Effective Protection of the Environment

A fundamental review and revision of the planning procedures and implementation of infrastructure in Hungary will be necessary. Two key areas need urgent attention:

- The energy supply situation, both domestic production and imports

- The progress of telecommunications projects.

The general objective should be to concentrate on tasks and projects that will help increase the productive potential of the economy. Technical assistance should be provided both by the World Bank and by officials from various European countries. It also appears necessary to upgrade the resources and quality of Hungarian construction companies to make them more competitive both in Hungary and abroad.

Effective protection of the environment is an urgent task in Hungary, both to correct the consequences of past errors and neglect and to prevent new neglect and new errors that could result from the expanding private sector and the economy in general. Protection of the environment is not anti-economic or anti-development. It is an important task to preserve resources and to improve the quality of life. It is not a luxury reserved for the most advanced industrialized economies. Protecting the environment is largely a public responsibility, although there are important dimensions that require a change of behavior by companies and by households. Environmental protection is an area where Hungary could and should take advantage, at the earliest date, of the possibilities of cooperation with the OECD countries.

19 Housing Policy

Hungarian housing policy had some successes in the past, but it has also been a source of major public deficits and of unequal treatment of various segments of the population. Today, Hungary needs a carefully designed new housing policy to improve the quite alarming state of much of the housing stock. This must be accomplished without tying up substantial additional resources or increasing social tensions and hardships. Housing policy reform and the development of a market in rental units would also reduce a major obstacle to people's movement between places and jobs.

A new housing policy should be tailored to the needs and conditions of Hungary. It should also be sufficiently flexible to take into account special problems. As the very example of Hungary demonstrates, the long-term economic and social costs of ill-conceived or rigid policies can be very high. Before adopting major changes, the Hungarian authorities should carefully examine the experiences of various European countries (such as, for example, the British policy of encouraging tenants of council houses to buy them at relatively low cost, which has notably improved the condition of the housing stock). Socially and politically acceptable measures should be found to affect similar results at minimal cost, either in real resources or in public money.

20 Personnel Training

Higher productivity and increased discipline are an essential ingredient of future economic success. The achievement of these objectives partly depends on the existence of positive and negative financial incentives and discipline at the workplace. Modern personnel training in the broadest sense is another key element.

For many years, training courses in Hungary were a means for increasing one's wages, whether or not they effectively increased productivity. Quality programs, innovation incentives, and similar attempts to raise productivity have had little visible impact and were in considerable disrepute.

Today, there are numerous signs of a greater interest in effective technical and business training in Hungary. Training courses aimed at the production level both for technical staff and workers are indispensable for raising quality and productivity. Personnel training could help change the lopsided wage and salary structures between production workers and civil servants.

Training courses are an area in which Western assistance can be obtained at relatively low cost. It seems important to obtain the cooperation of international companies, banks, and financial institutions. These programs should be directed in particular at young people and should not be limited to office workers and managers. Rewards of higher wages should not be given for the extra qualification, but for the increased productivity it makes possible.

EPILOGUE

The original report from which this book was drawn was completed in January 1990 under the title *Hungarian Economic, Financial and Monetary Policies: Proposals for a Coherent Approach.* Except for minor corrections of style and changes aimed at avoiding confusion (e.g., when speaking of the "current" government), no significant alterations were made in the text of the original report.

Regardless of the exceptional speed and the fundamental nature of the political changes that have occurred since early 1990 in Hungary, East Germany, and other European countries (including the Soviet Union), the conclusions and recommendations for action by Hungary and the OECD countries presented in this book remain valid and highly topical.

Since the completion of the report, its conclusions have been presented in a series of private conversations to officials in Hungary and to national and international officials in the OECD countries. They agreed that implementing such a set of recommendations would greatly enhance the chances for success of transforming the Hungarian economy and of integrating it into the European and world economy.

General readers and decision makers, both inside and outside Hungary, will note three sets of recent developments that reinforce the conclusions of this book. These developments concern (1) the opportunity offered by the historic political changes in Hungary during the spring of 1990, (2) the example of the economic and monetary union between the two Germanys and Hungary, and (3) the evolution of Western policies toward the formerly communist countries of Eastern and Central Europe.

1 **The outcome of free elections in Hungary: A smooth transition toward democracy**

A fundamental change in the political system and a smooth transition toward a Western type of democracy have been recognized as the single most important condition of a successful transformation of the Hungarian economy into a dynamic market economy. This condition was largely fulfilled with the Hungarian elections in the spring of 1990. In fact, the first free elections since the 1940s resulted in a clear (and probably stable) centrist majority and an opposition that, for the most part, is likely to be loyal and constructive.

In outlining the program of his government, new Prime Minister Jozsef Antall defined the creation of a social market economy in Hungary as the fundamental long-term economic objective of his government. He also stressed that Hungary wants to honor its external financial obligations and to maintain its good relations with the international financial community. Promoting the development of the private economy and integrating Hungary into the European and world economies are among several basic goals on which there is broad consensus between the majority and opposition parties in the newly elected parliament. Although membership in the European Community is the long-term objective, the Hungarian government appears keenly interested in establishing and maintaining close cooperation not only with the member countries of the European community, but also with other OECD governments.

2 Hungary and the example of Germany

The conclusions and recommendations in this study were formulated before the approach for the economic and monetary union of Germany began to take shape, and well before the initial announcement of plans for such a union. However, from an economic standpoint, the approach adopted in Germany is powerful confirmation of the correctness of the approach suggested in this book.

In terms of economic policy requirements, the situation in Germany shows that the task of reconstruction, the fundamental change from a communist to a free market economy, and the integration with the Western economies cannot be achieved solely through domestic efforts, nor through official or private foreign credits, nor on the basis of externally defined austerity programs.

The current German approach incorporates the same three ingredients, though on a much larger scale, of the postwar European Recovery Program (i.e., the Marshall Plan):

- Clear definition of a medium-term goal (liberalization and, of course, establishment of the social market economy)

- Close cooperation with and official advice from other countries

- Generous external financial assistance.

The agreement for German economic and monetary unification also shows a clear understanding of the need for an approach that balances the tasks of the private sector and the responsibilities of the public sector, in both the financial and organizational arenas. The agreement also illustrates the principle that without an efficient government there can be no efficient market economy. Furthermore, it recognizes that creating a market economy on the ruins of forty years of socialism requires not only market discipline but also public generosity.

On a more technical level, the need to separate the current management of the economy from the financing of the long-term reconstruction and development of the economy, a central thesis throughout the recommendations of this book, is shown in the creation of the German Unity Fund and the fund for consolidating the productive sector (i.e., institutions that are similar to the bank proposed in this book).

Finally, in addition to hastening the development of a market economy in what used to be one of the most orthodox communist countries in Europe, the sponsorship and remarkable solidarity shown by West Germany will guarantee East Germany's integration into the Western economy and into all Western economic and political organizations.

To expect assistance and cooperation on a similar scale for Hungary or the other former communist countries in Europe would be unrealistic. The expectations of the Hungarians themselves are also more modest: although they had been trying to get rid of the socialist economic system for a much longer time than the East Germans, they do not expect to reach West German living standards as rapidly.

At the same time, it is important to realize that, even if East Germany is a "special case" (for essentially ethnic reasons), the same underlying economic logic applies to the transformation of at least some of the other Eastern European economies, and certainly to Hungary. As mentioned above, such was the conclusion of this report, which has been confirmed by the implementation of similar logic in Germany, the country with the most successful record of economic and monetary reforms and policies in the postwar period.

The Western nations as a whole will benefit by translating the German experience of solidarity and realization of the need for economic integration into a comprehensive approach for Hungary and the other former communist countries. To miss this opportunity would be not only a major economic policy error, but also a serious political mistake.

While Germany is rightly occupied with its own huge task of unification, it is probably the country whose people have the most immediate understanding of the issues at stake in Hungary. Therefore, the responsibility falls to the other OECD countries to ensure that, at a time when East Germany will be benefitting from "an unprecedented Marshall Plan," action in favor of Hungary and the other Eastern European countries is limited neither to official and private lending nor to admonitions for domestic austerity.

3   **Hungary and the Group of 24: Hope for a constructive outcome**
On the whole, the author finds reason to hope that the Group of 24 (the OECD countries) will rise to the challenge of close and innovative cooperation with Hungary. The actions and the direct or indirect promises of members of the Group of 24 concerning Hungary's economic integration into the European Community are particularly encouraging. Hungary's determination to avoid a debt crisis, commendable in itself, also could have an important demonstration effect outside Europe. It is recognized, at least privately, that Hungary should not be economically and financially penalized as a result of its determination to honor its external obligations and to avoid unilateral measures concerning its interest payments. There is need for *ex ante*, rather than *post ante*, financial help (not limited to commercial loans) from the public sector in the OECD countries; this necessary contribution to economic and monetary stabilization in Hungary constitutes a relatively small amount in absolute terms.

Although some observers who lack historical perspective and direct experience in implementing deep-seated economic reforms seem to favor a *tabula rasa* approach, most Western officials are encouraged by Hungary's clear determination to adopt the model of a social market economy.

Officials in the OECD countries frankly admit that they currently have no blueprint for assisting Hungary and the other Eastern European countries. Yet the consensus favors a case-by-case approach and close and pragmatic cooperation among the various Western countries and organizations concerned. Thus, there is reason to hope that Hungary will be a success story.

Otto Hieronymi
Geneva
June 1990

APPENDIX

Table I *Hungarian Legislation 1987–1989*

	Political Policy	Economic Policy	Entering into force	Law or Regulation
1.		Land-ownership	September 1, 1987	1987, Law I
2.	Change of Criminal Code		July 26, 1987	1987, Law III
3.	Change of Criminal Code		July 26, 1987	1987, Law IV
4.		**VAT**	**January 1, 1988**	**1987, Law V**
5.		**Personal Income Tax**	**January 1, 1988**	**1987, Law VI**
6.	Reorganization of Ministries		December 18, 1987	1987, Law VII
7.		**Banking Reform**	**January 1, 1987**	**1987, Law IX**
8.	**Amendment to Constitution**		**January 1, 1988**	**1987, Law X**
9.	New Principles in Law-Creation		January 1, 1988	1987, Law XI
10.	Review of Laws and Regulations, created before 1960		January 1, 1988	1987, Law XII
11.		Public Transportation		1988, Law I
12.		Co-operatives		1988, Law II
13.		Agricultural Co-operatives		1988, Law III
14.		Food Production		1988, Law IV
15.		Acceptance of 1987 State Budget		1988, Law V
16.		**Corporation Act**	**January 1, 1989**	**1988, Law VI**
17.		Modification of Act V. 1987 General Turnover Tax		1988, Law VII
18.		Modification of Act Vi. 1987 Personal Income Tax		1988, Law VIII
19.		**Corporate Profit Act**	**January 1, 1989**	**1988, Law IX**
20.		Modification of Corporate and Personal Income Tax		1988, Law X
21.		National Technical Development Fund		1988, Law XI

Table I   *Hungarian Legislation 1987–1989 (continued)*

	Political Policy	Economic Policy	Entering into force	Law or Regulation
22.	Modification of Criminal Code			1988, Law XII
23.	Modification of Civil Code			1988, Law XIII
24.		Modification of Law IX. 1987		1988, Law XIV
25.		Taxes on Commercial Buildings		1988, Law XV
26.	Reorganization of Ministries			1988, Law XVI
27.		1989 Budget		1988, Law XVII
28.		Amendment of Corporate Income Tax		1988, Law XVIII
29.		Amendment of Personal Income Tax Law		1988, Law XIX
30.		Amendment of Special Tax Laws		1988, Law XX
31.		Modernization of the Social Security System		1988, Law XXI
32.		Minor amendment to SSS		1988, Law XXII
33.		Formation of skilled workers		1988, Law XXIII
34.		**Foreign Investments' Act**	**January 1, 1989**	**1988, Law XXIV**
35.	Amendment to Civil Code			1988, Law XXV
36.	National Defense			1988, Law XXVI
37.	**Amendment to Constitution**		**January 24, 1989**	**1989, Law I**
38.	**Freedom of Associations**		**January 24, 1989**	**1989, Law II**
39.	**Freedom of Assembly**		**January 24, 1989**	**1989, Law III**
40.	Freedom of Assembly (Amendment)		March 14, 1989	1989, Law IV
41.		Labor Law	March 25, 1989	1989, Law V
42.		Domestic Trade	March 25, 1989	1989, Law VI

Table I *Hungarian Legislation 1987–1989 (continued)*

Political Policy	Economic Policy	Entering into force	Law or Regulation
43.	Strikes	April 12, 1989	1989, Law VII
44. Amendment to Constitution		May 26, 1989	1989, Law VIII
45. Reorganization of Ministries		May 26, 1989	1989, Law IX
46. Amendment to Civil Code		May 26, 1989	1989, Law X
47. Amendment to Electoral Law		May 26, 1989	1989, Law XI
48. Striking of Law 1953/I. about Stalin		May 26, 1989	1989, Law XII
49.	**Transformation of Corporations**	**July 1, 1989**	**1989, Law XIII**
49.	Transformation of State Enterprises	July 1, 1989	1989, Law XIII
50.	Transformation of Co-operatives	July 1, 1989	1989, Law XIV
51. Amendment of Civil Code		June 15, 1989	1989, Law XVI
52. Popular Referendum		**June 15, 1989**	**1989, Law XVII**
53.	Amendment of 1989 Budget	June 22, 1989	1989, Law XVIII
54.	Amendment of Land Act	June 22, 1989	1989, Law XIX
55.	Amendment of Re Agr. Co-operatives	June 22, 1989	1989, Law XX
56.	Amendment of Land Act	July 7, 1989	1989, Law XXI
57. National Defense		July 7, 1989	1989, Law XXII
58. Amendment to Civil Code		July 7, 1989	1989, Law XXIII
59.	1988 Budget	July 7, 1989	1989, Law XXIV
60. Amendment of Penal Code		October 15, 1989	1989, Law XXV
61. Amendment to Penal Code		October 15, 1989	1989, Law XXVI
62.	Amendment to Corporate and Personal Income Tax	October 15, 1989	1989, Law XXVII
63. Passports		October 19, 1989	1989, Law XXVIII

Table I *Hungarian Legislation 1987–1989 (continued)*

Political Policy	Economic Policy	Entering into force	Law or Regulation
64. Emigration and Immigration		October 19, 1989	1989, Law XXIX
65. Discontinuation of Workers' Militia		**October 21, 1989**	**1989, Law XXX**
66. Amendment to Constitution		**October 23, 1989**	**1989, Law XXXI**

* Bold type indicates principal legislation

** year   [1986]   1987   1988   1989
    no. of laws   [4]   **4** + 8 = 12   **3** + 23 = 26   **7** + 24 = 31

Table II   *The Structure of the GDP, 1987–1989*
(Current Prices, Billion HF)

	1987	1988	1989 (est)
1. Industry	402	431	519
2. Building Industry	92	96	96
3. Agriculture and Forestry	189	204	282
4. Transportation, Post and Telecommunication	95	100	118
5. Commerce	128	126	129
6. Utilization of Water resources	17	17	21
7. Other material products	13	15	19
8. *Services	174	218	260
9. Others	116	204	220
10. Total, All Sectors	1,226	1,411	1,665
11. Private Consumption	779	861	1,040
12. Public Consumption	126	160	141
13. Subtotal, Consumption (C), lines 11+12	905	1,021	1,181
14. Investments	304	298	382
15. Change in Stocks	24	54	50
16. Subtotal, Investments (I), lines 14+15	328	352	432
17. Subtotal, Domestic (C+I), lines 13+16	1,233	1,373	1,613
18. Netto Exports (+), Imports (−)	−7	+38	+52
19. Total, Absorbtion	1,226	1,411	1,665

*Including public health, social, cultural, community services, administration

Memoranda Items

M1. Consumer Price Index	100	117	138
M2. GDP at Constant 1987 Prices	1,226	1,206	1,207
M3. Exchange Rate 1 US$=HF	47	50	62

Table III The Structure of the GDP, 1987–1989, at Comparative Prices (Percent)

	1987	1988	1989 (est)
Sources (Y)			
1. Industry	36.7	36.5	36.5
2. Building industry	6.9	6.6	6.6
3. Agriculture and Forestry	19.5	20.4	20.4
4. Transportation, posts and telecommunication	9.0	9.1	9.1
5. Commerce	9.6	8.6	8.6
6. Utilization of water resources	1.4	1.5	1.5
7. Other material activities	1.4	1.3	1.3
8. Services	15.5	16.0	16.0
9. Total, all sectors	100.0	100.0	100.0
Utilization (C + S)			
10. Private Consumption	64.0	62.7	62.7
11. Public Consumption	10.8	11.3	11.3
12. Subtotal, Consumption (lines 10+11)	74.8	74.0	74.0
13. Investment, exchange in stocks	25.9	24.6	24.6
14. Change in stocks	−0.7	1.4	1.4
15. Subtotal, Investment (lines 13+14)	25.2	26.0	26.0
16. Total, Utilization (C+S)	100.0	100.0	100.0

Table IV *Hungarian Budgets, 1987–1989*
(Billion HF)

	1987	1988 (expected)	1989 (planned)
Revenues			
1. Profit and Income Taxes	152	174	221
2. Incomes of Social Security	149	182	214
3. Tax on wages	43	13	8
4. Property tax	25	6	6
5. Turnover taxes	208	318	300
6. Taxes on international trade	43	46	55
7. Other tax incomes	12	7	2
8. Revenues of institutions	54	57	59
9. Revenues deriving from property	6	6	4
10. Other revenues	50	57	66
11. Total revenues (lines 1+10)	742	866	935
Expenditures			
12. Material expenditures	243	304	365
13. Interest payments	32	43	27
14. Production and Price Subsidies	217	180	137
15. Social Security	155	215	257
16. Investments	100	106	101
17. Other expenditures	25	38	63
18. Total expenditures (lines 12+17)	772	886	950
Deficits	−30	−20	−15
Memoranda Items			
M1. GDP	1,226	1,411	1,665
M2. Budget in % of GDP	63	63	57

Table V Hungary's Balance of Payments in Convertible Currencies, 1987–1989 ($US Million)

	1987[a]	1988[a]	1989[a,b]	1990
1. Exports	5,078	5,794	6,700	
2. Imports	5,075	5,124	6,000	
3. **Trade Account (lines 1+2)**	3	670	700	
4. Freight and Insurance, net	−308	−300	−325	
5. Travel, net	368	41	−600	
6. Investment income, net	−924	−1,048	−1,200	
7. Govt. expenditures, net	−52	−76	−80	
8. Other current receipts, net	−36	7	10	
9. Unrequested transfers, net	102	114	125	
10. **Service account (lines 4+9)**	−850	−1,262	−2,070	
11. **Current account (lines 3+10)**	−847	−592	−1,370	
12. Changes in assets, net	−97	−38	−30	
13. Changes in liabilities, net	1,177	315	658	
14.*Changes in short-term capital, net	−1,137	154	−10	
15. **Capital account (lines 12+14)**	−57	431	618	
16. **Balance of Payment (lines 11+15)**	−904	−161	−752	
17. **International Reserves as of January 1**				
18. Gold-doreign exchange	3,639	2,478	2,194	1,457
19. External Assets	3,657	4,357	4,087	4,072
20. Total IRs (lines 17+18)	7,296	6,835[c]	6,281[d]	5,529
21. **External Debt as of January 1**				
22. Gross External Debt	15,086	17,738	17,349	17,502[e]
23. International Reserves	7,296	6,835	6,281	5,529
24. Net External Debt	7,790	10,903	11,068	11,794

[a]Lines 1 through 16 encompass the entire year.
[b]Estimated; includes errors and omissions.
[c]Includes $US 433M in not properly explained monetary movement.
[d]Includes $US −393M in unexplained monetary movement.
[e]The adjusted figures, announced by Prime Minister Németh on 11/21/89, in $US billion: Gross external debt, 40; International reserves, 6; Net external debt, 14.

Table VI   *Transferable Ruble Balance of Trade*
(Billion HF)

	1988 Jan–Jun	1989 Jan–Jun	Change
TOTAL	+ 2,3	+ 10,1	+ 7,8
USSR	+ 5,8	+ 10,2	+ 4,4
East Germany	− 1,9	− 1,2	+ 0,7
Checoslovakia	+ 0,3	+ 1,0	+ 0,7
Poland	− 0,3	+ 0,3	+ 0,5
Rumania	− 1,0	+ 0,2	+ 1,2

Table VII   *Non-Ruble Foreign Trade Balance*
(Billion HF)

	1988 Jan–Jun	1989 Jan–Jun	Change
Socialist countries	+ 2,5	+ 7,3	+ 4,8
Developed market economies	− 4,6	+ 2,3	+ 2,3
European Community	− 6,1	− 4,0	+ 2,1
Developing countries	+ 4,5	+ 4,4	− 0,1
TOTAL	+ 2,4	+ 9,4	+ 7,1
($US million)	+ 47	+ 146	+ 98

Table VIII   *Balance of Payments in Convertible Currencies
($US Million)*

	1988 Jan–Aug	1989 Jan–Aug
In convertible currencies		
Exports	3,504.3	4,145.5
Imports	3,306.7	3,921.2
Trade balance	197.6	224.3
Travel credit	371.0	483.3
debit	252.9	855.5
net	118.1	− 372.2
Investment income, net	− 669.0	− 806.0
Current account balance	− 568.1	− 1,171.5
Capital inflows	1,546.8	1,790.0
Capital outflows	1,457.1	997.1
Overall balance	− 130.9	− 416.3
In nonconvertible currencies		
Exports	2,870.1	2,817.7
Imports	2,893.2	2,419.6
Trade balance	23.1	398.0
Current account balance	32.6	581.1
Overall balance	− 161.2	352.6
Total convertible and nonconvertible currencies		
Exports	6,374.4	6,963.2
Imports	6,199.9	6,340.8
Trade balance	220.7	622.3
Current account balance	− 535.0	− 591.0
Overall balance	− 30.3	− 63.7

Table IX *Main Items of the Balance Sheet of
the National Bank of Hungary, 1987–1988
(Billion HF)*

	1987	1988
TOTAL ASSETS	1,167	1,225
Medium and long-term advances, loans, and credits	558	886
to banks	− 385	− 403
to enterprises and budgetary institutions	− 37	− 37
to state budget	− 136	− 446
Short-term advances, loans, and credits	− 145	− 124
to banks	− 138	− 115
Other assets	− 302	− 53
TOTAL LIABILITIES	1,168	1,225
Fixed deposits	718	771
to banks	− 711	− 769
to residents	− 70	− 63
to nonresidents	− 641	− 705
Sight deposits and accounts	164	148
to banks	− 128	− 114
to residents	− 68	− 53
to nonresidents	− 59	− 61

Table X   *Price Categories of Consumer Purchases, 1976, 1980, and 1988*
(Percent)

Item	1976		1980		1988	
	Authority determined	Free	Authority determined	Free	Authority determined	Free
Food	75	25	72	28	28	72
Beverages and tobacco	77	23	73	27	—	100
Clothing	40	60	20	80	—	100
Durables and hardware	47	53	40	60	—	100
Automobiles	89	11	100	—	100	—
Household chemicals	22	78	23	77	9	91
Furniture	81	19	1	99	—	100
Cultural articles	25	75	25	75	7	93
Heating materials	100	—	95	5	95	5
Construction materials	75	25	50	50	—	100
Pharmaceuticals	98	2	98	2	91	9
Total retail trade	64	36	50	50	20	80
Other household energy	100	—	100	—	100	—
Water	100	—	100	—	100	—
Free farmers' market	3	97	—	100	—	100
Other services	52	48	45	55	18	52
Building of flats	22	78	22	78	1	99
TOTAL consumer purchases	58	42	45	55	20	80